Canada
YEAR IN REVIEW 2004

Conservative Leader Stephen Harper is
questioned by media in Drummondville, Que.,
during the 2004 federal election campaign.
(Frank Gunn/CP)

Alexandre Despatie competes during the men's three-metre springboard preliminaries at the 2004 Summer Olympics. (Adrian Wyld/CP)

Canada
YEAR IN REVIEW 2004

Editor: Patti Tasko
Photo Editor: Ron Poling

John Wiley & Sons Canada, Ltd.

Library and Archives Canada Cataloguing in Publication

Canadian Press
         Canada : year in review 2004 / The Canadian Press.

ISBN 0-470-83529-X

 1. Canada—History—1963—Pictorial works. 1. Title.
FC59.C3455 2004   971.07'1   C2004-905912-2

Production Credits:

Cover design: Ian Koo & Mike Chan
Interior text design: Adrian So R.G.D. & Mike Chan
Printer: Transcontinental Printing

Printed in Canada

10 9 8 7 6 5 4 3 2 1

CONTENTS

PART 1: The Year That Was

PART 2: National News and Politics

PART 3: The Regions of Canada

Pg. 32

Pg. 50

Part 4: Business and Finance

Pg. 58

Part 5: Sports

Part 6: Crime and Punishment

Brutal murders of little girls shock Toronto

"Shattered" former MP Svend Robinson given conditional discharge for stealing ring

Judge sentenced for sexually assaulting young prostitutes who appeared in his court

Nine Hells Angels and associates convicted of total of 26 criminal charges

Air India bombing trial slow to shed light

Notorious teen murder trial ends in mistrial; Kelly Ellard denies she killed fellow teen

The sweet scent of money smells a lot like pot to grow-op owners

Part 7: Health, Science and Lifestyles

Grade 3 student from New Brunswick becomes Canada's first "bionic" boy

Low-carb craze leads to new products on store shelves

Trans fat = bad fat = bad publicity

Two Canadian teams enter contest to launch private spacecraft

Online lotteries in Canada spark controversy

Same-sex marriages—and divorces—cause controversy

Battle over genetic seed patent goes to Supreme Court

Bare bellies everywhere

Spam: E-mail nightmare lurks in desktops everywhere

Worries about West Nile disease fade as summer passes

Fears about flu end quickly, but long-term planning continues

More Canadians turn to marijuana

Survey of youth contradicts image of troubled, unruly teenagers

Part 8: Canada Around the World

Canadian Forces safeguard security in Kabul

New prime minister abroad

Canadian Forces general revisits Rwanda horror at UN tribunal

Death of Canadian photojournalist strains Canada-Iran ties

Canada stays out of Iraq invasion

Former prime minister delivers eulogy at former U.S. president's funeral

Canadian veterans remember D-Day

U.S. air force reprimands pilot who bombed Canadians

Canadian troops keep peace in post-Aristide Haiti

Pg. 130

Part 9: Arts & Entertainment

Part 10: Fairly Odd News

Canada's biggest lottery winner shy about collecting winnings
Winnipeg's Professor Popsicle takes icy plunge on Letterman's talk show
Bees kill heifer on southwestern Ontario farm
Back-country break-in artist eats foods, drinks booze, then tidies up
Maybe they like maple syrup: Number of UFOs being spotted in Canada increases
Too many earthworms threaten alpine environment near Calgary
Speedy golf-ball-stealing rodents drive Edmonton golfers squirrelly
Woman reunited with runaway cat after 18 years on the lam
This butter tastes too good to go down the drain
Man caught stealing cheese ordered to produce a painting for the courts
Grenade discovered in Yellowknife backyard detonated by military bomb squad

Part 11: Passages

Alex Barris, 81
Gerald Bouey, 83
Reva Brooks, 90
Norman Campbell, 80
Micheline Charest, 51
Frank Cotroni, 72
Doug Creighton, 75
Frances Hyland, 77
Eric Kierans, 90
Brian Linehan, 58
Keith Magnuson, 56
Harrison McCain, 76
Jack McClelland, 81
Guido Molinari, 70
Moe Norman, 75
Betty Oliphant, 85
Toni Onley, 75
Claude Ryan, 79
Mitchell Sharp, 92
Robert Stanfield, 89
Hugh Charles Trainor, 87
Percy Wickman, 63
Fay Wray, 96

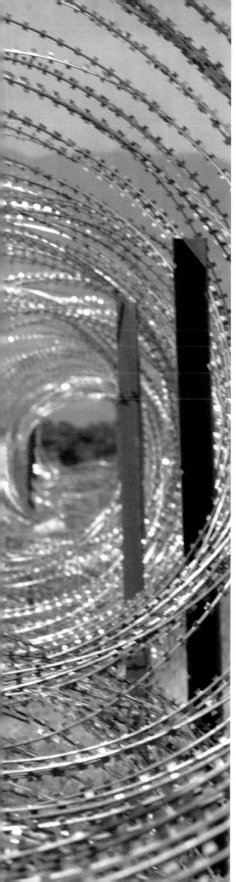

PART 1
The Year That Was

Introduction

The reporters and photographers at The Canadian Press have the privilege of occupying front-row seats to watch history in the making. Every day, they observe, first-hand, the people and events that shape Canada and change the lives of its residents.

Often there is nowhere our journalists would rather be. Who wouldn't want to be rinkside as Canada's hockey team wins the World Cup? Or on the Canadian Walk of Fame watching comedian Jim Carrey mug for the cameras? Or at the Canadian Open for the dramatic playoff between Mike Weir and Vijay Singh?

Many times, however, it is hard to keep watching. It could be at the funeral of a murdered young girl, as her parents collapse in grief. It might be in a courtroom as a teen matter-of-factly recounts how he beat another teen to death. Or it might be in a dusty tent in Afghanistan, watching as Canadian doctors attempt to help a young boy suffering from a medical condition that could be easily treated in a more advanced country.

But it is the job of journalists to keep their eyes—and camera lenses—firmly focused on the story. No blinking allowed.

At CP, we take pride in covering every corner of this big country. From our daily news report, gathered by our journalists who live and work across the country, we have gathered together the most memorable stories and images from a year of Canadian news. *Enjoy your front-row seat.*

◀ Pte. Paul Bilton of Gander, Nfld., one of the troops Canada sent to Haiti to help bring stability to the country, works on a wire barrier surrounding the Canadian base at the Port-au-Prince airport in March 2004. (Ryan Remiorz/CP)

◀ Vancouver swimmer Mark Johnston dresses up as Captain
Canada to cheer on his teammates in the pool during the
2004 Athens Olympics. (Paul Chiasson/CP)

A gas station on the New Maryland Highway, north of Fredericton,
passes judgment on spiralling gasoline prices in May 2004.
▼ (Stephen MacGillivray/*Fredericton Gleaner*)

▲ David Miller addresses council after being sworn in as Toronto's new mayor in December 2003. Promising a new era for the city, Miller won the job in a hard-fought election after incumbent mayor Mel Lastman retired. (Rick Madonik/*Toronto Star*)

Smoke rises from a six-alarm, deliberately set fire that ▶ destroyed the Toronto Island Yacht Club in June 2004. (David Cooper/*Toronto Star*)

◄ Canada's largest airport, Pearson International in Toronto, shows off its new Terminal 1, which opened to passengers in April 2004. (Tobin Grimshaw/CP)

Judoist Nicolas Gill takes souvenir photos of the Parthenon in Athens. The next day he carried Canada's flag at the opening
▼ ceremonies for the 2004 Olympics. (Paul Chiasson/CP)

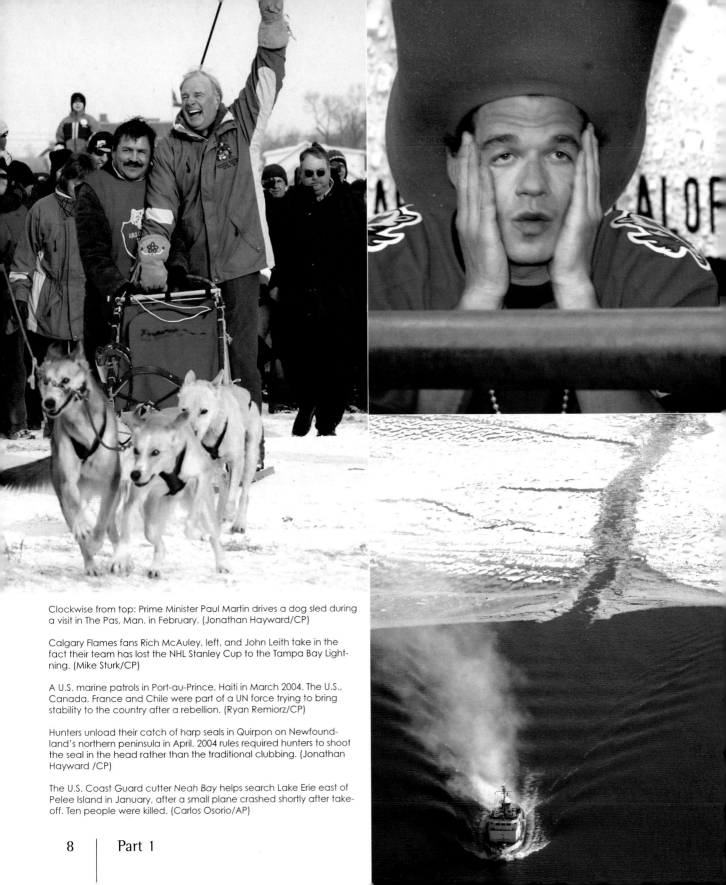

Clockwise from top: Prime Minister Paul Martin drives a dog sled during a visit in The Pas, Man. in February. (Jonathan Hayward/CP)

Calgary Flames fans Rich McAuley, left, and John Leith take in the fact their team has lost the NHL Stanley Cup to the Tampa Bay Lightning. (Mike Sturk/CP)

A U.S. marine patrols in Port-au-Prince, Haiti in March 2004. The U.S., Canada, France and Chile were part of a UN force trying to bring stability to the country after a rebellion. (Ryan Remiorz/CP)

Hunters unload their catch of harp seals in Quirpon on Newfoundland's northern peninsula in April. 2004 rules required hunters to shoot the seal in the head rather than the traditional clubbing. (Jonathan Hayward /CP)

The U.S. Coast Guard cutter Neah Bay helps search Lake Erie east of Pelee Island in January, after a small plane crashed shortly after take-off. Ten people were killed. (Carlos Osorio/AP)

Montreal Canadiens goalie Jose Theodore during an outdoor game against the Edmonton Oilers at Commonwealth Stadium in Edmonton in November 2003. (Tom Hanson/CP)

Oposite: Brad Richards of the Tampa Bay Lightning after his team beats the Calgary Flames to win the Stanley Cup on June 7, 2004. (Ryan Remiorz/CP)

Adam van Koeverden crosses the finish line to win a gold medal in kayaking at the Summer Olympics in Greece. (Andre Forget/Canadian Olympic Committee)

Opposite top: The Dalai Lama receives an honorary degree from Simon Fraser University in Vancouver in April. (Richard Lam/CP)

Opposite bottom: A Canadian veteran catches a ride through the streets of St-Aubin-sur-Mer in France during celebrations marking the 60th anniversary of D-Day. (Adrian Wyld/CP)

Opposite right: Marie-Hélène Prémont of Chateau Richer, Que., winds her way through the forest to win the silver medal in the women's mountain bike cross country event at the 2004 Games. (Paul Chiasson/CP)

PART 2
National News and Politics

Election 2004: Liberals salvage minority

Prime Minister Paul Martin battled back from the edge of an electoral abyss on June 28 to retain the Liberals' grip on power with a minority win. The victory gave his party its fourth consecutive mandate, but it faced the prospect of needing help from other parties to hold on and run the country.

The Liberals won 135 seats, down from 176 in the last election in 2000. It was a long way from the mighty Jean Chrétien majorities but good enough to beat Stephen Harper's Conservatives, who took 99 seats. The NDP won 19 seats, while the Bloc Québécois ran away with Quebec, taking 54 of the province's 75 ridings. Independent Chuck Cadman won in the B.C. riding of Surrey North after campaigning from a cancer ward following the loss of the Conservative nomination. The results meant that Martin needed the support of 20 opposition MPs to operate.

The election result, which saw the Liberals win 37 per cent of the vote compared to 30 per cent for the Conservatives, flew in the face of campaign opinion polls that had indicated the parties were locked in a dead heat. It also pointed to the success of a relentless Liberal assault on Harper as a right-wing bogeyman who would run roughshod over minority rights and impose socially conservative mores on the country.

Liberals win minority

Here is a look at the number of seats won in each province and territory in the 38th federal election:

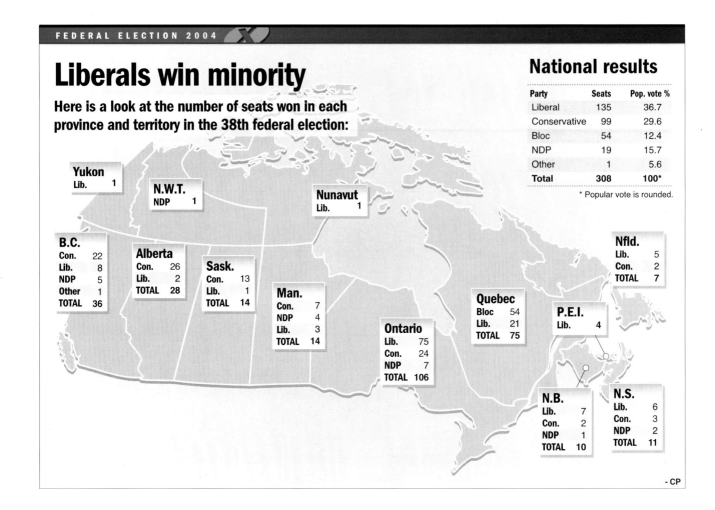

National results

Party	Seats	Pop. vote %
Liberal	135	36.7
Conservative	99	29.6
Bloc	54	12.4
NDP	19	15.7
Other	1	5.6
Total	**308**	**100***

* Popular vote is rounded.

Yukon
Lib. 1

N.W.T.
NDP 1

Nunavut
Lib. 1

B.C.
Con. 22
Lib. 8
NDP 5
Other 1
TOTAL 36

Alberta
Con. 26
Lib. 2
TOTAL 28

Sask.
Con. 13
Lib. 1
TOTAL 14

Man.
Con. 7
NDP 4
Lib. 3
TOTAL 14

Ontario
Lib. 75
Con. 24
NDP 7
TOTAL 106

Quebec
Bloc 54
Lib. 21
TOTAL 75

Nfld.
Lib. 5
Con. 2
TOTAL 7

P.E.I.
Lib. 4

N.B.
Lib. 7
Con. 2
NDP 1
TOTAL 10

N.S.
Lib. 6
Con. 3
NDP 2
TOTAL 11

- CP

Harper managed a breakthrough in Ontario that had eluded Conservatives since 1988, stealing 24 seats from the Liberals. The Tories also dominated in the West. The NDP got about 16 per cent of the popular vote, the Bloc 12 per cent and the Green party four per cent.

It was a bittersweet outcome for Martin. The result was a blow when seen from the perspective of a few months before the vote, when heady Liberals were blithely predicting a huge majority. But it was also likely sweet relief after a devastating drop in opinion polls that pointed to a Conservative upset over Liberals stung by a scandal over government sponsorship money and hobbled by an unpopular budget brought down by their Grit cousins in Ontario.

Martin said Canadians sent the government an "unmistakable" message. "Canadians expected, and expect, more from us and as a party and as a government we must do better, and we will—I pledge that to you tonight," he told supporters in his home riding of LaSalle-Émard, Que. (Martin O'Hanlon, CP)

◀ Conservative Leader Stephen Harper addresses rally in Charlottetown on May 25. (Adrian Wyld/CP)

Bloc Québécois Leader Gilles Duceppe listens during a press conference in
▼ Rosemere, Que. on May 31. (Francois Roy/CP)

▲ NDP Leader Jack Layton rides bus to his campaign headquarters in Toronto on May 26. (Andrew Vaughan/CP)

◀ Paul Martin and his wife Sheila at the Liberal leadership convention in Toronto in November 2003. (Jonathan Hayward/CP)

Joe Who becomes Joe Retired

Joe Clark wound up his long career in Parliament still bitterly lamenting the union of his beloved Progressive Conservative party with the former Canadian Alliance. The man known as Joe Who?, Honest Joe and, in later years, the elder statesman of the now defunct Progressive Conservatives, spent his last day in the raucous chamber that has defined much of his life.

Clark, 64, split from the new Conservative Party of Canada and didn't seek re-election. But on May 13, 2004, there was no mention of his bitter rift with former colleagues as tributes flowed, along with some tears. Clark's voice broke when he thanked his wife, Maureen McTeer, and daughter Catherine for their steadfast support as they beamed from the public gallery.

First elected to Parliament in 1972, Clark served as his party's leader twice, from 1976 to 1983 and then again beginning in 1998. At age 39, he served briefly as Canada's youngest prime minister before his minority government collapsed on a confidence vote in 1979.

Deputy Prime Minister Anne McLellan praised Clark for leading the Canadian crusade to end apartheid in South Africa while foreign minister in Brian Mulroney's cabinet. He was also hailed as a progressive and distinguished parliamentarian.

Clark was not the only MP to leave federal politics before the June election. Also saying goodbye to life on the Hill were Liberals Charles Caccia, former defence minister Art Eggleton and former human resources minister Herb Dhaliwal, and Conservative Elsie Wayne, the popular former mayor of Saint John. Veteran Liberal Sheila Copps, meanwhile, left politics, but not intentionally—she lost a bitter nomination battle to Tony Valeri after their Hamilton-area ridings were redrawn into one. (Sue Bailey, CP)

▲ Prime Minister Paul Martin jokes around with Gabriel McGraw, 8, who is wearing an Acadian flag hat, during campaigning for the federal election in St. Stephen, N.B. (Tom Hanson/CP)

▲ Acadian singer Jeanne (Doucet) Currie of Annapolis Royal, N.S., at the Acadian Congress at Grand Pré on August 15. (Andrew Vaughan/CP)

Acadians reunite at site of 1755 deportation

The third international reunion to celebrate Acadian culture attracted thousands of visitors from around the world to Atlantic Canada in the summer of 2004. The celebrations were centred in Grand Pré, N.S., the spot where a British order to deport all Acadians was read in 1755.

On the green hillside beside the tiny chapel at Grand Pré, as many as 10,000 people took holy communion during a French mass during the reunion's final day. As the choir sang the theme song for the congress, "Je reviens au berceau de l'Acadie/I'm returning to the cradle of Acadia," there were tears among those in the crowd, many of whom wore the red, white and blue of the Acadian flag. For so many who stood for hours in the blazing heat the congress was about finding family, blood-related or not.

"We met at the last congress in Louisiana," said Agathe Brunet of Orleans, Ont., as she stood next to her Cajun friend Lilly Chauvin from Houma, Louisiana. The women said they formed a bond at the congress, which helped them reconnect with a culture that can be traced back to their common ancestors who farmed the fields around Grand Pré. "When you say Grand Pré, I have shivers," Brunet said. "It's so special, this place. It's where it all started."

After Britain won the wars in North America during the 18th century, it rounded up more than 11,000 French-speaking farmers and their families and deported them because they refused to swear allegiance to the Crown. The Acadians scattered along the eastern United States and France, with many ending up in Louisiana, where they became known as Cajuns. Others went into hiding in the Maritime woods. (Susan Aitken, CP)

Canadian arrested for terrorism demands answers

▲ Maher Arar and his wife Monia Mazigh at a news conference in Ottawa on November 4, 2003. (Tom Hanson/CP)

Maher Arar was a communications technology consultant, a resident of Ottawa and a Canadian citizen, when his life took a drastic turn in September 2002. During an airport stopover in New York as he returned from a family vacation in Tunisia, he was taken into custody by American authorities and grilled about alleged links to the al-Qaida terrorist network. Less than two weeks later, he was shackled and flown to Jordan aboard a private plane, then transferred to a prison in his birthplace of Syria.

Arar, 33, who denied any involvement in terrorism, said he was beaten, tortured and forced into giving false confessions while locked in a tiny, grave-like cell for more than 10 months. Once he was finally returned to Canada, he demanded a public probe into his imprisonment. "The only way I will be able to move on and have a future is if I find out why this happened to me," he said. "The only way I can learn is to have all the truth come out in a public inquiry."

The federal government appointed Justice Dennis O'Connor to conduct a public inquiry into how and why Arar was deported and imprisoned, including what involvement Canadian authorities may have had. O'Connor, who began the hearings in mid-2004, had a big job—all potential evidence before the commission, including more than 20,000 documents, had to be assessed for national security claims before any witnesses could testify.

Sponsorship scandal drags down new government

It started with a report by Auditor General Sheila Fraser that criticized unaccounted-for spending in a $250-million federal sponsorship program designed to raise the federal profile in Quebec and fight separatism after the 1995 referendum on sovereignty. Fraser said that some ad firms—many with close ties to the Liberal party—that received money appeared to do little or no work to earn their fees. In other cases, she said, the documentation was so scanty it was impossible to say whether Ottawa got value for its money.

From there, the scandal snowballed to include several government departments and Crown corporations that had also paid ad agencies for services. Heads of Crown corporations were suspended, including André Ouellet of Canada Post, Via Rail's Marc LeFrançois and Michel Vennat of the Business Development Bank of Canada. Jean Pelletier, CEO of Via, was fired after he called Olympic gold medallist Myriam Bédard a "pitiful" single mother when she said she was forced from her job at Via after asking questions about the sponsorship program. Alfonso Gagliano, who was public works minister when the sponsorship program was set up, was recalled as ambassador to Denmark and fired.

A parliamentary committee, pushed by opposition MPs relishing the thought of publicly questioning Liberal appointees in an election year, held hearings into the affair. Prime Minister Paul Martin, anxious that his new government not be tainted by allegations that dated back to Jean Chrétien's regime, asked

Auditor General Sheila Fraser and former public works minister Alfonso Gagliano on Parliament Hill on March 18. (Tom Hanson/CP)

RCMP to investigate. Eventually, two central figures in the scandal, Chuck Guité and Jean Brault, were each charged with six fraud-related charges. Martin also called an inquiry, under Justice John Gomery of Quebec Superior Court, which began hearings in the fall of 2004.

Fraser's findings also prompted a followup audit at Canada Post that led to the resignation of its president, Ouellet. The audit reported that the long-time Liberal insider and career politician had spent $2 million on travel and hospitality over eight years without supporting receipts; that virtually all 83 of Canada Post's "special hires" outside normal rules between 1996 and 2003 involved people Ouellet had recommended; and that he had intervened in the tendering process for three contracts worth a total of $35 million. Ouellet defended his actions point-by-point but said the politics of a minority government made it impossible for him to stay.

Farmer Hermann Volk of Metchosin, B.C. stands in his broiler barn, emptied of its 22,000 chicks because of avian flu fears. (Darren Stone/*Victoria Times Colonist*)

▲ Canadian Food Inspection Agency official visits farm in Abbotsford, B.C. (Richard Lam/CP)

Bird flu clears Fraser Valley of all its fowl

It took a drastic measure, but it was a potentially catastrophic situation. About 17 million chickens were slaughtered in the Fraser Valley in British Columbia in the spring of 2004 in an attempt to wipe out the avian flu virus.

The cull started in mid-February and took about three months, leaving empty barns and destitute farmers in its wake. It included birds in large-scale farming operations and backyard flocks. Even pets were not saved from the slaughter. Chicken farmers lost millions of dollars in the crisis, and faced a long process of decontaminating their barns before they could get back into production. But by the end of May the valley was declared free of the virus.

The crisis had far-reaching consequences. Even the Canadian Kennel Club had to move its field trials out of the Fraser Valley because there weren't enough domesticated game birds for the dogs to find.

Birds from flocks that tested positive for the virus were incinerated, composted or put into landfills, while birds testing negative were slaughtered for market. There are several different strains of avian flu and the strain found in the Fraser Valley, while devastating to birds, is not a serious threat to humans.

Bird flu first broke out in Asia in early 2004, and at its height decimated flocks, as 100 million chickens were killed to stop its spread.

Cattle graze in the foothills of the Canadian Rockies near Longview, Alta. (Jeff McIntosh/CP)

Canada's beef farmers continue to be held hostage by mad cow disease

The discovery of a single case of mad cow disease on an Alberta farm in 2003 continued to have devastating reverberations for Canada's beef farmers more than a year later.

When one Alberta cow was diagnosed with bovine spongiform encephalopathy, or BSE, more than 30 countries immediately closed their borders, including the United States, which is the primary market for most of Canada's cattle business. Many cattle producers saw decades of equity evaporate in 12 months as the U.S. continued to keep its border closed to the crucial trade in live cattle, and open only to certain cuts of beef.

BSE eats holes in the brains of cattle; humans who eat the contaminated beef can develop a deadly form of the disease.

Before the BSE discovery, cattle moved freely back and forth across the border. After the discovery of BSE and the halt in trade, American investors began coming up to Canada in droves, buying up cheaper livestock in Canadian feedlots from cash-crunched producers. "If there's any profitability in those animals once they're ready to go to market and the border opens, it's all heading south," said Ron Axelson of the Alberta Cattle Feeders.

The shift to American ownership was one of the major changes to the landscape of southern Alberta, where much of Canada's live cattle industry is located. It has resulted in huge frustration for Canadian producers. "We have no problem with them up here purchasing our cattle, but open up the border so we can take our fat cattle down there, too," said Rick Paskal, who operates feedlots near Picture Butte in southern Alberta and is a spokesman for the group Canadian Cattlemen for Fair Trade.

Tired of the political stalemate between the two countries on the issue, the group launched a multi-million-dollar claim against the U.S. government in August in a bid to force the reopening of the border to live cattle. "Our rights have been violated. We have no marketplace here in Canada . . . we've got a wreck coming here," said Paskal.

The mad-cow crisis was a major factor in the dramatic drop in the net cash income of Canadian farmers to the lowest level in more than 25 years. Net cash income—the amount of money taken in by farmers after expenses—fell more than 43 per cent in 2003 to $4.2 billion, the lowest level since 1977.

"These are tough times. Let's face it," said George Brinkman, an agriculture economics professor at the University of Guelph in Ontario. "The farmers we've got out there are some of the best. They have survived the 1980s when we had tough times . . . and now they are really getting hit with another set of factors outside their control."

New privacy commissioner, smaller lunch cheques

She may be Canada's privacy commissioner, but Jennifer Stoddart wants everyone to know how much she spends on lunch.

Stoddart replaced George Radwanski in the top civil-service job late in 2003, five months after he resigned over spending habits that included lavish meals and travel. In a scandal that enveloped Ottawa

▲ George Radwanski at a news conference in June 2003. (Jonathan Hayward/CP)

for weeks, Radwanski earned the dubious honour of becoming the first Canadian to be found in contempt of Parliament because he provided misleading information about his expenses.

In her first months on the job, Stoddart took a different approach. Canadians interested in how much she was spending on travel and hospitality could check the privacy commission's website, where such expenses as a working lunch with a privacy computer specialist—cost $11.30—were listed. (Radwanski once claimed a dinner for two at $444.49.) In total, in her first month on the job Stoddart charged $54.22 in hospitality spending—taxes included.

With Stoddart's appointment, Canada's privacy office could move away from the expenses controversy and back to its mandate of protecting the privacy of Canadians. One of her first priorities was to reassure businesses scrambling to understand and comply with new privacy legislation. The new law requires all businesses across Canada to follow rules that aim to protect the personal information of their customers and employees.

New military helicopters finally on their way

They were a long time coming, but the Canadian Forces finally got a commitment that it would get new helicopters. Defence Minister Bill Graham announced the $5-billion project to buy 28 bargain-priced Sikorsky Cyclones to replace Canada's geriatric fleet of Sea King helicopters in front of a squad of Sea King pilots and crew—most of them far younger than the aircraft they flew—at a military air base near Halifax.

Graham said the Cyclone, the military version of the Sikorsky S-92, "represents the right helicopter for the Canadian Forces at the best price for Canadians." The military, despite previous misgivings, appeared to be on side, saying politics didn't affect a decision that was more than 25 years in the making.

> Jean Chrétien declared in 1993 that the helicopters were "Cadillacs" the nation couldn't afford.

Critics said the process was ridiculously slow and badly flawed. In the end, the government chose a helicopter with no military track record, built by U.S.-based Sikorsky Aircraft Corp. It was touted as the less-expensive option when compared with its main rival, the larger, three-engine EH-101 Cormorant, built by a British-Italian consortium.

The announcement closed a saga that began in the 1980s, when the Defence Department set out to replace the CH-124 Sea King, also a Sikorsky product. The matter could have been settled when Brian Mulroney's Conservative government ordered 50 Cormorant-built helicopters in 1992. But the $5.8-billion contract was cancelled by former Liberal prime minister Jean Chrétien, who declared in the 1993 election campaign that the helicopters were "Cadillacs" the nation couldn't afford. His move cost taxpayers $500 million in penalties and became a lightning rod for those who argued the Liberal government was set on destroying Canada's military. (Michael Tutton, CP)

▲ Stephen Butler prays while attending the Dalai Lama's afternoon prayers in Toronto. (Colin Corneau/CP)

◄ Actress Goldie Hawn introduces the Dalai Lama to a packed audience in Vancouver. (Sam Leung/CP)

Exiled Tibetan leader welcomed to Canada

During a 17-day visit to Canada, the Dalai Lama became the first Tibetan spiritual leader in history officially welcomed by a Canadian prime minister. He was also honoured and entertained by several of the country's luminaries and fêted by celebrity devotees from south of the border, including actors Richard Gere and Goldie Hawn.

The Dalai Lama has headed a government in exile in Dharamsala, India, since fleeing Tibet in 1959 after a failed uprising against China, which has occupied the former country since 1951.

In Vancouver, where his visit began April 17, 2004, thousands of people lined up for hours to see him and fellow Nobel Peace Prize laureates Archbishop Desmond Tutu and Iranian rights activist Shirin Ebadi. "He is about one of a very few people who can fill Central Park in New York with adoring devotees who respond to him as if he were a pop star," Tutu, the leader of the Anglican diocese of South Africa, said about his longtime friend. In a musical tribute to the religious icon hosted by Hawn in Vancouver, the Hollywood actress called his message of forgiveness, kindness and love "a fabulous cocktail for peace on earth."

During his visit to Ottawa, local-born singer Alanis Morissette performed for the spiritual leader before an audience of 10,000, introducing the 1989 Nobel Peace Prize winner as a man of "vision, warmth, humour and grace." But the highlight for supporters was their spiritual leader's meeting with Paul Martin, the first sitting Canadian prime minister to so honour the head of Tibetan Buddhism.

During their brief meeting, Martin and his guest avoided the hot-button issue of Tibetan autonomy within China and spoke instead about human rights in the region and elsewhere. The meeting drew the ire of Beijing, which considers the Dalai Lama a renegade separatist, and left Martin straddling a fine balance—asserting Canada's right to make its own decisions while being careful to limit any offence to China, Canada's fourth-largest export market.

The Tibetan leader stressed repeatedly throughout his Canadian visit that he was not seeking independence for the homeland he fled 45 years ago. His goal is cultural and religious autonomy for Tibet within a stable, thriving China, he said.

The final stop of his visit was Toronto, where he completed an initiation ceremony into the spiritual practices of Tibetan Buddhism. About 7,000 people, including dozens of robe-clad monks, attended the ritual to initiate hundreds of devotees that was marked by prayers, chants and teachings from the Tibetan spiritual leader.

For Tina Petrova, a practising Buddhist, seeing the Dalai Lama in her hometown was summed up in one word: "Wow." She then remarked, "He just instills in one a sense of deep calmness and serenity, and you can just feel his purity of heart." (Sheryl Ubelacker, CP)

Canada: Americans' favourite drug pusher

Thousands of Americans looking for prescription drugs have been turning to Canada, e-shopping over the border for price savings ranging from 30 to 80 per cent. The phenomenon has spawned a billion-dollar fight that pits health professionals against each other and raises questions of ethics versus profit margins.

try, several U.S. cities and states pushed to import Canadian drugs en masse for their employees, prisoners or pensioners.

As the business has increased, so have forces against it, including the major global drug companies (known as Big Pharma) and in Canada the doctors who speak for and regulate other doctors. Big Pharma said they needed to charge the higher prices to cover the costs of researching new drugs, and some of them stopped selling to pharmacists who export to the United States, citing safety as the issue. That raised concerns of drug shortages in Canada.

The main concern is that a prescription written by a U.S. doctor must be signed by a Canadian doctor so it may be filled by a Canadian pharmacist. While

Big Pharma stopped selling drugs to some pharmacists who export to the United States.

About 130 Internet pharmacies in Canada, most in Manitoba but also scattered across Alberta, British Columbia and Ontario, feed the U.S. customers their prescription drug fix through the mail and courier services. In 2004, the Internet drug business was estimated to be worth $1 billion a year, with some companies filling 7,000 orders a week. The industry reportedly started when two young pharmacists fresh from the University of Manitoba started selling nicotine patches over the Internet. When that proved lucrative, they expanded their business.

Almost all Americans using Internet pharmacies are uninsured or under-insured. Federal price controls on prescription drugs make Canadian prices cheaper than those in the United States. Despite opposition from U.S. drug regulators and the indus-

Canadian doctors, who are paid between $7 and $15 per prescription, have access to the patient's medical history, they are signing off on medication for someone they have never seen let alone treated. "It's absolutely appalling practice to prescribe a medication for a patient when you have no idea who the patient is," said Dr. Bill Pope, registrar of the College of Physicians and Surgeons of Manitoba.

Supporters of Internet pharmacies chalked up the concerns of Big Pharma to thinly disguised corporate greed, and Americans using the pharmacies said they would not be able to afford the drugs otherwise. (Michelle MacAfee, CP)

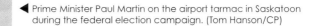
◀ Prime Minister Paul Martin on the airport tarmac in Saskatoon during the federal election campaign. (Tom Hanson/CP)

U2 singer Bono was an unconventional guest speaker at the Liberal convention that picked Paul Martin as leader in November 2003. He said he agreed to the ▼ gig because of Martin's record on supporting foreign aid. (Frank Gunn/CP)

PART 3
The Regions of Canada

Members of the Mowachaht-Muchalaht First Nation watch
Luna in Mooyah Bay, west of Gold River, B.C., in June 2004.
(Richard Lam/CP)

BRITISH COLUMBIA

Luna: Just a lonely whale or the spirit of dead chief?

A rambunctious but lonely killer whale named Luna became the focus of a high seas tug-of-war between northern Vancouver Island aboriginals and federal fisheries scientists in the summer of 2004.

Fisheries officials tried to capture the 1,360-kg whale as part of an effort to reunite him with his pod off southern Vancouver Island. They were concerned Luna's increasingly friendly behaviour—bumping up against boats and hanging out near the dock at the tiny community of Gold River—would eventually lead to tragedy. There were reports of Luna getting in the way of a float plane and vigorously rubbing himself against boats.

But local aboriginals intervened, taking to the ocean in canoes to lure Luna away from the capture pen. After a week of tension, the capture was put off and the two groups agreed to jointly monitor the four-year-old killer whale.

The Mowachaht-Muchalaht believe Luna embodies the spirit of their late chief, Ambrose Maquinna, who said he would return to them in the form of a whale after he died. Only days after the chief's death three years ago, Luna appeared in the Gold River area.

The attempts to capture Luna and the efforts of the aboriginals to prevent it drew international attention. Federal Fisheries Minister Geoff Regan received letters from organizations in 10 countries asking the government to abandon the plan to capture Luna. (Dirk Meissner, CP)

Jim Clarkson of the Teamsters Union supports striking Health Care Employees
▼ Union members, in Richmond, B.C., in May 2004. (Richard Lam/CP)

Defiant B.C. union faces big fine for illegal strike

The union representing British Columbia's hospital employees was fined $150,000 for an illegal strike in the spring of 2004 after a judge found the public pain and anxiety caused by the strike to be "incalculable." It was the highest levy against a union for illegal job action in the province's history and ranked near the highest fines ever levied against a union in Canada.

"What is clear is that the loss represented by the pain, suffering, stress, anxiety and just plain inconvenience to the public, wrought by these activities, is incalculable," said Justice Robert Bauman.

The Hospital Employees Union began a legal strike on April 25, then defied government legislation ordering the hospital employees back to work a few days later. The union accepted the judge's offer of letting them donate the fine to hospital charitable foundations. "Our fight was never with the court," said union spokesman Chris Allnutt. "Our fight is with the mean-spirited provincial government. We'll continue that fight."

The strike by the province's 43,000 hospital support workers gripped the province for a week. Thousands of surgeries and diagnostic procedures such as MRIs and ultrasounds were cancelled. The provincial Liberal government passed back-to-work legislation April 29 that featured a 15 per cent wage and benefit rollback, which further infuriated the union and prompted members of other unions to walk off their jobs and call for a general strike. In the face of this threat, union and government officials negotiated late into the night to come up with an agreement that kept the wage and benefit cuts, but provided more guarantees against contracting out work. (Terri Theodore, CP)

▲ Ian Hardy and his father Gord sit with their car during flooding in Edmonton. (Perry Mah/*Edmonton Sun*)

▲ People wade through the flooded West Edmonton Mall parking lot. (Jason Franson/*Edmonton Sun*)

THE PRAIRIES
Parts of Edmonton under water or buried in hailstones after punishing storm

For northern Alberta, summer 2004 was one of soggy misery. The lowest point came in mid-July when a sudden and vicious hailstorm hit Edmonton, causing tens of millions of dollars in damage and flooding parts of the city, including the West Edmonton Mall, Canada's largest shopping complex. The 800-store complex was evacuated after holes were ripped in the mall's roof. "There was like a waterfall coming down," said shopper Arte Jolly. "As we walked away we heard things smashing behind us. I thought it was a good time to leave." There was a sprawling traffic jam outside the mall as motorists fought through waist-high pools of water to get out.

Elsewhere, the deluge swamped major intersections and closed arterial roads, forcing cars into bumper-to-bumper gridlock on side streets. Mountains of hail lined boulevards, brushed up against fences and turned lawns into muddy snowbanks. Snowplows were used to keep the drifts of hail at bay.

Municipal politician guilty of faking stalking complaint

It seemed an unbelievable story when it was first reported: a city alderwoman from Lethbridge, Alta., had been abducted while on city business in Montana. It turned out it was.

Dar Heatherington, 41, made headlines in 2003 when she mysteriously disappeared in Montana. She surfaced three days later in Las Vegas, alleging she had been abducted and sexually assaulted—a story discounted by U.S. investigators.

But that wasn't the end of the soap opera-like story. She was later charged with mischief by Lethbridge police, who had been investigating her complaints that she was being stalked and suggestive phone calls and lurid letters were coming to her family home. During her trial she maintained her innocence, but provincial court Judge Peter Caffaro sided with evidence showing she had written the letters herself. He sentenced Heatherington to eight months of house arrest and 12 months of curfew in September 2004.

During sentencing, a sobbing and shaking Heatherington appeared to be unsteady on her feet and was given permission to sit in the prisoner's dock. Caffaro said the fact Heatherington had served her community as an alderwoman and did not have a criminal record worked in her favour. "In this case we have public mischief but no specific victim. The victim is the municipality of Lethbridge," said Caffaro.

Lethbridge Mayor Bob Tarleck said city residents had already put the episode behind them. "I wish Mrs. Heatherington the best of luck as she and her family move beyond this." (Bill Graveland, CP)

◀ Dar Heatherington and her husband David arrive at the Lethbridge, Alta., courthouse in June 2004. (Jeff McIntosh/CP)

Brutal blizzard causes state of emergency in Nova Scotia and P.E.I.

Halifax resembled an ice-age wasteland after a record 92 cm of snow fell on February 19, 2004, producing a thick, smothering blanket that prompted the Nova Scotia government to declare its first-ever province-wide state of emergency—something not even hurricane Juan could muster just four months before.

"I've lived here all my life and I've never seen this kind of thing," said Ian MacFarlane as he and his wife shovelled waist-deep snow from their suburban driveway.

On Prince Edward Island, where at least 69 cm fell on Charlottetown, a state of emergency was also declared. Thousands in both provinces lost power. "This is a good, old-fashioned nor'easter," said Jack McAndrew from his Cornwall, P.E.I., home. "It's not a sissy storm. It's a storm with muscles."

The blizzard, the fiercest of a brutally cold but largely tame winter, closed schools, government offices and businesses throughout the region. It also cancelled flights and elective hospital surgeries and made highways impassable. Described as a weather bomb by Environment Canada, the storm obliterated Halifax's one-day snowfall record of 50.8 cm, which was set in 1944. (Steve MacLeod, CP)

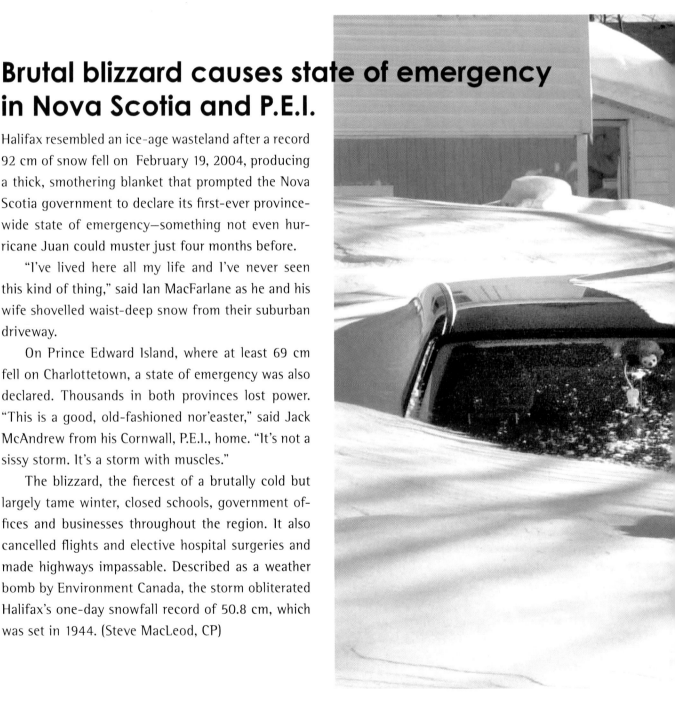

Cindy DeDieu and Chrissy Rogers dig Rogers' car out of the snow in Dartmouth, N.S., in February 2004. (Darrell Oake/*Halifax Daily News*)

ATLANTIC CANADA

▲ Sam Kelly, president of St. John's and district council for CUPE, loads strike signs into a truck. (Jonathan Hayward/CP)

▲ Danny Williams, premier of Newfoundland and Labrador, holds copy of government offer to striking public service unions on a picket line. (Gary Hebbard/*St. John's Telegram*)

Newfoundland orders its striking public workers back on the job

Newfoundland's Conservative government resorted to back-to-work legislation in April to force 20,000 striking civil servants to end a bitter, almost month-long strike over wages and benefits.

The government, saying it couldn't afford to give the public-sector workers the raises they wanted, imposed a two-year wage freeze, followed by a 2 per cent increase in 2006 and 3 per cent in 2007. Wayne Lucas, CUPE's Newfoundland president, minced no words when he criticized the offer from Premier Danny Williams. "Danny Williams, the miserable louse, wants to give you less benefits than what we struggled for the last 30 years," Lucas said. "He couldn't get it at the negotiating table, so he crept in the back door and will introduce a bill which will legislate concessions for the first time in our history into the collective agreement."

Finance Minister Loyola Sullivan said the strike had to end because of the pressure being put on the health system, schools, and other government services. A major snowstorm also hit during the strike, which caused extra problems as snowplow drivers were on the picket line. (*St. John's Telegram*)

CUPE president Wayne Lucas, left, and NAPE president Leo Puddister, after announcing their unions would strike. (Jonathan Hayward/CP)

Labrador Inuit vote overwhelmingly in support of new region called Nunatsiavut

Inuit in Labrador voted overwhelmingly in 2004 to accept a historic land claim that will create Nunatsiavut, a region of self-government in northern Labrador that is larger than Ireland.

The agreement gave Labrador Inuit outright ownership of 15,800 square km of land, with the right to control resources, forge laws, and control education and social services. They also got limited resource and management rights over another 56,700 square km of land.

The deal includes a commercial fishery and a detailed plan for self-government. Inuit who live outside Nunatsiavut will maintain rights within the region and will have representation in government.

The Nunatsiavut legislature will be located in Hopedale, Labrador, and the administration in Nain. Both Inuit and non-Inuit residents will be able to vote for and serve as councillors on community governments, but non-Inuit will not be able to serve as community leaders, who will have a seat in the regional government.

◄ Union members picket outside the Health Sciences Centre in St. John's, Nfld., in April 2004. (Jonathan Hayward/CP)

QUEBEC

Firebombing of Jewish school causes widespread outrage

In an attack that made headlines across Canada and overseas, the library of a Jewish school in Montreal was destroyed by a firebomb on April 5, 2004. A note left at United Talmud Torahs' elementary school said the fire was in retaliation for Israel's strike that killed Hamas leader Sheikh Ahmed Yassin. No one was injured, but the school estimated it would cost about $300,000 to replace books destroyed in the fire.

Actor Russell Crowe, shooting a movie in Toronto, was among the dozens of callers who offered moral support and pledged money to help rebuild the library. Prime Minister Paul Martin and Quebec Premier Jean Charest condemned the fire, with Martin calling it "a cowardly and racist act" against all values espoused by Canadians. Five people were arrested and charged with the firebombing in May.

◀ The library at the United Talmud Torah elementary school the morning after it was firebombed. (Ryan Remiorz/CP)

Thousands of people march in downtown Quebec City on July 22, 2004, to protest a CRTC decision to refuse the licence renewal of radio station CHOI. (Stevens Leblanc/CP)

Quebec radio station inspires fans, detractors

CHOI Radio, a popular radio station in Quebec City, inspires either love or hate, it seems. Some people hated it enough to complain to radio regulators for years about off-colour humour and comments by on-air personalities. But after the Canadian Radio-television and Telecommunications Commission yanked its licence, thousands of fans turned Parliament Hill into an outdoor concert to show their support for the station.

The demonstrators ranged from families with young children to grey-haired seniors to teens in tight black CHOI-FM T-shirts. Hundreds of people came from Quebec City in buses. "We think freedom of speech is very important and we don't want to see the government telling us what we have the right, or not the right, to listen to," said Marie-Claude Gagne. Rallies were also held in Quebec City.

In a ruling criticized by politicians, the CRTC refused to renew CHOI's licence and ordered it to stop broadcasting at the end of August 2004. CHOI was rebuked for jokes about psychiatric patients being gassed, about the breasts of a local TV personality, and for describing African exchange students as the children of cannibals and plunderers. The station was later given a reprieve and allowed to stay on air while it appealed the decision.

ONTARIO

Flooding in Peterborough leaves some without homes for weeks

It took weeks for the residents of the central Ontario city of Peterborough to dry out their possessions and salvage what remained after a flash flood made the city a disaster area in July.

Water-damaged furniture and personal belongings piled up on city streets as residents cleaned out their homes following the flood, which filled about 800 basements and caused millions of dollars in damage.

The flood came after Peterborough was hit with a record amount of rain. Sewers backed up and a local creek overflowed, putting about one-third of the city under water.

Michael Allan pedals his bicycle on a Peterborough street after 161 millimetres of rain fell in the city. (Clifford Skarstedt/*Peterborough Examiner*)

Toronto Police Service rocked by charges of corruption

Some members of the police force in Canada's largest city found themselves on the other side of the booking desk in 2004. An RCMP investigation into organized crime led to a series of charges against Toronto police officers. In one case, several officers were accused of tipping off bar owners about liquor licence investigations and claiming they could influence the reduction or withdrawal of penalties in exchange for payment. In another case, six members of a Toronto drug squad were charged with criminal offences ranging from drug dealing to shaking down witnesses to falsifying search warrants. The unit was disbanded after the charges were laid. And four other Toronto police officers were charged under the Ontario Police Services Act on 14 counts, including discreditable conduct.

Chief Julian Fantino, a controversial figure who inspires either fierce loyalty or intense dislike among Torontonians, insisted that the few bad eggs did not reflect on the overall integrity of his force. But Fantino himself found his time on the force coming to an end when the city's police board decided not to renew his contract after March 2005. Although it is unusual for chiefs to serve two terms in Toronto, Fantino, 62, had indicated he wanted to.

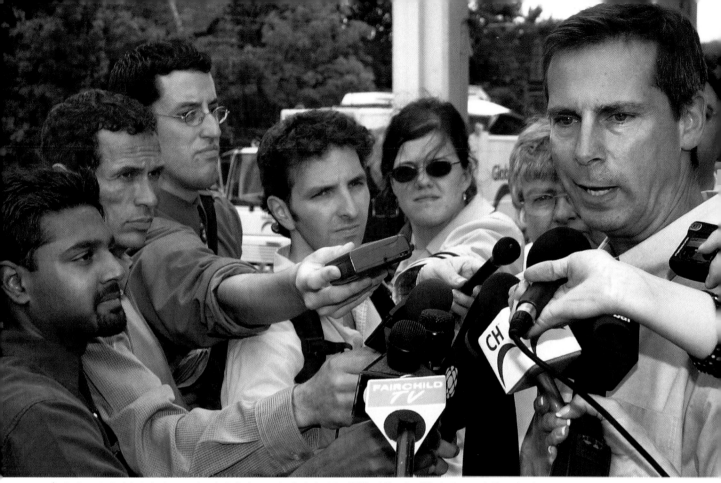

▲ Dalton McGuinty talks to reporters in Peterborough, Ont., in July. (Clifford Skarstedt/*Peterborough Examiner*)

Ontario government battered by new health premium

Ontario Liberal Leader Dalton McGuinty promised not to raise taxes or run a deficit during his 2003 election campaign. So McGuinty took a lot of grief when he did just that in his first budget, introducing a controversial health-care premium that ranged from $60 to $900 annually per taxpayer.

The new premier said he had no choice but to break his promises because of the nearly $6-billion deficit left by the previous Conservative government. But his critics were not so forgiving, and McGuinty was forced to spend chunks of his summer on what opposition politicians called the "Dalton damage control summer tour," a road trip around Ontario designed to help shore up the damaged credibility of the rookie Liberal government. (Keith Leslie, CP)

THE NORTH
Elections in North return one leader while another retires

A new era in the politics of the Northwest Territories began when Stephen Kakfwi decided not to contest his seat in November 2003 territorial elections. In various cabinet seats and as premier, Kakfwi had seen his territory through the events that will define it for the next generation and beyond: division with Nunavut; the opening of the diamond industry; and the coming of the gas pipeline.

He was replaced by Joe Handley under the consensus government system used in the N.W.T. and Nunavut, with the premier and cabinet chosen by legislature members following a general election. Handley, a 60-year-old Metis who grew up in the northern Saskatchewan bush, was such a strong contender that nobody bothered to run against him.

Handley, who had served as deputy minister in several departments before being elected to the N.W.T. legislature in 1999, made it clear quickly that his mandate was to ensure that northerners see some social benefits from the territory's resource-driven economic boom. "A key principle of our social agenda should be to assist people to be independent and responsible for themselves and their families." The new premier also promised to renew the fight with Ottawa for control over northern resources and the revenue that flows from them. Currently, all royalties from northern diamond production and natural gas belong to the federal government.

In neighbouring Nunavut, meanwhile, religon and cultural values became election issues alongside the usual concerns about housing, jobs and health in a bruising February 2004 election for premier. When the dust settled, the incumbent, 39-year-old lawyer Paul Okalik, had defeated challenger Tagak Curley in a secret ballot held among the 19 legislature members. Okalik acknowledged that he will have to address concerns that his first government failed its Inuit constituents, who represent 85 per cent of the population.

Many of Nunavut's more than 26,000 residents viewed the election as their first chance to grade the government on its performance since the territory was formed in April 1999, after decades of land claims negotiations with the federal government. In its first five years, the fledgling government missed its targets for Inuit employment levels within the bureaucracy, which is made up largely of people from southern Canada.

Then there was the divisive issue of human rights. Socially conservative MLAs, including Curley, denounced Nunavut's Human Rights Act, passed in 2003, for outlawing discrimination based on sexual orientation, suggesting that it would lead to same-sex marriages in the territory. Curley, strongly associated with Nunavut's burgeoning evangelical Christian community, said the act was incompatible with traditional Inuit culture. During their campaigns, many of the winning candidates promised to repeal the section protecting gays and lesbians.

Business and Finance

PART 4

(Jonathan Hayward/CP)

I Am Also American: Molson–Coors merger?

Molson, Canada's largest brewer and one of the country's best-known companies, announced a plan in 2004 to join forces with another family-run brewing icon in the United States to create the Molson Coors Brewing Co., the world's fifth-largest beer producer. But in the weeks after the initial announcement, it looked like the merger might go flat. The market's reaction to the news was lukewarm, and Molson chief Dan O'Neill speculated that he might not have the votes needed to win shareholder approval. And there were rumours that a group led by former vice-chairman Ian Molson would come forward with a different offer.

Montreal-based Molson was founded in 1786 by John Molson, making it one of Canada's oldest companies. After finding success with beer, Molson went on to also found Montreal's first commercial steamship business, railway, luxury hotel and theatre. The Molson name was linked with many landmarks including Molson's Bank, which eventually merged with the Bank of Montreal, and the Montreal Canadiens hockey club. Molson often promoted its nationality with ad campaigns that featured such mottos as "I Am Canadian."

No matter the fate of the Coors-Molson merger, it seemed inevitable that a wave of consolidation in the global beer industry would eventually mean Molson would stop being Canadian—at least wholly Canadian-owned. It happened a few years earlier to Labatt, its chief Canadian competitor, when it became part of Belgian beer giant Interbrew. (Steve Erwin, CP)

Air Canada focuses on cost control as key to staying in business

Air Canada continued to fight its way back to commercial viability in 2004, releasing a plan detailing how it hopes to operate profitably after restructuring. The plan included a reduced mainline fleet of smaller aircraft, several thousand fewer workers and no negotiations with unions on wages until at least 2006. "The foundation of the new business plan is a competitive cost structure," Air Canada said.

Canada's premier airline needed significant cost cuts and had to secure major financing agreements in order for it to emerge from restructuring. It negotiated deals with all of its unions on labour cost reductions and restructured its aircraft leases. The company set up a new corporate structure—creating a holding company similar to its U.S. rivals—and got hundreds of millions of dollars in new financing from a big German bank and New York investment company.

While Air Canada tried to come to grips with its problems, relations with its closest Canadian rival, WestJet Airlines, got nasty amid allegations of corporate espionage between the two companies. WestJet, meanwhile, spread its wings beyond its western base and added many new routes, which put a gravitational pull on its profits. Small no-frills airlines such as Jetsgo and Canjet also popped into the mix, attracting customers with discount pricing and saucy advertising. (Steve Erwin, CP)

Frank Dunn, then president and CEO of Nortel Networks, at Nortel's annual meeting in 2003. (Chris Wattie/CP)

Nortel: The roller-coaster ride continued

◀ An Air Canada Airbus A-321 takes off while a WestJet Boeing 737 taxis on the ground at Calgary International Airport. (Larry MacDougal/CP)

Nortel Networks, Canada's flagship technology company, has been both an unprecedented success story and a scourge on the market. There was more bad news in April 2004. The company fired CEO and president Frank Dunn and two other senior executives after an internal review revealed its 2003 profit was only about half the $732 million (in U.S. dollars) it had originally reported.

Regulators ordered Nortel to restate its financial results for each quarter in 2003 and for earlier periods, including 2002 and 2001. The Brampton, Ont.-based company also faced probes by Canadian and U.S. regulators, along with dozens of class-action lawsuits by aggrieved investors. The U.S. Attorney's office in Dallas was conducting a criminal investigation. Former CEO Dunn told analysts repeatedly in late 2002 and early 2003 that Nortel would achieve profitability by the second quarter of 2003.

In the absence of hard numbers, Nortel's roller-coaster ride on the stock market continued, depending on the content of the updates new CEO Bill Owens was ordered by regulators to provide every other week. In July 2004, for instance, he said Nortel would focus on cost controls to boost profits and stock prices went up. In the next update, he warned the company was falling short of its cost targets. Down went share prices. For Nortel, the ride wasn't over.

Record prices provide respite for Canada's steelmakers

It was a turbulent year for Canada's steel makers. Three companies, Montreal-based Ivaco Inc., stain-less-steel maker Slater Steel Inc. and Hamilton-based Stelco Inc., the largest steel producer in Canada, found themselves in creditor protection, driven there by years of low steel prices and mounting losses.

But even as Stelco was being granted protection from creditors in January, the steel market was turning, driven by ravenous demand from China—both for steel and for the coal, iron ore and other materials needed to make it. As China grabbed steel from around the world, prices soared to record high levels virtually overnight, especially in North America.

The price jump was too late to save Slater, which was liquidated, and Ivaco, which was sold to a Chicago-based turnaround specialist. Canada's healthier steel companies, Hamilton-based Dofasco Inc., Algoma Steel Inc. in Sault Ste. Marie, Ont.—which restructured twice in the last decade—and Ipsco Inc. of Regina, all posted healthy profits on the back of the higher prices. Stelco benefited as well with its second-quarter 2004 financial results representing its strongest performance since 1998.

That wasn't enough, however, to prevent it from seeking government help to deal with a massive $1.25-billion pension shortfall or to keep it from insisting to approximately 7,000 unionized employees that they would have to make major concessions if the company was going to survive.

Enron scandal ensnared Canadian banks

The financial fraud that led to the collapse of Enron Corp. stretched into Canada, as three of the country's biggest banks found themselves drawn into the probe of the U.S. energy trading giant. The Royal Bank, Toronto-Dominion Bank and CIBC were all named in reports after a court-appointed examiner concluded they "aided and abetted" the accounting debacle at Enron.

CIBC settled for US$80 million with the Securities and Exchange Commission in December over the bank's alleged role in the energy trader's collapse. The three banks were also added to the list of defendants in a US$25-billion class-action lawsuit against Enron.

Conrad Black loses his flagship newspaper, but publishes noteworthy book

He battled his own shareholders in court and published a biography on former U.S. president Franklin Delano Roosevelt. All in all, it was quite a year for Canadian-born financier Conrad Black.

In November 2003, Black, one of Canada's best-known business tycoons, was forced to step down as CEO of his publishing company, Hollinger International, amid allegations that he and his affiliates had improperly collected more than US$32 million in "non-compete" fees connected with the sales of Hollinger properties. The controversy did not stop a defiant Black from attending a book-signing in Toronto for his FDR biography, where he faced off against a crowd of reporters.

Black's battles with his directors and their shareholders continued throughout 2004. A group of independent Hollinger International directors sued him, claiming he owed the company millions in improper payments. He sued back for defamation, claiming they had made him a "loathing laughingstock."

The directors sold Black's flagship newspaper, Britain's *Telegraph*, to a British company owned by the Barclay brothers after conducting a public auction. (Earlier, he had tried to sell it to the same brothers in a side deal that was blocked by court order.) Black tried to hold up the sale so that it could be subjected to a shareholder vote, but a judge threw out his argument.

Black may not have been able to win his directors, shareholders or judges over, but one group was supportive: book reviewers were complimentary about his FDR biography.

If it was connected to housing, it was hot

Above: Condominiums and apartments go up on the old Expo site in Vancouver. (Don Denton/CP)

Opposite page: Conrad Black, left, and lawyers leave court in Wilmington, Del., in February 2004. (Bradley Bower/AP)

Not only did the asking prices for new houses take the biggest jump in 14 years in 2004, it was the strongest year for new home construction since 1987. And the same conditions that created a red-hot housing market—ultra-low interest rates, steady job creation and an improving economy—also fuelled runaway cottage sales in many areas across Canada. The year-over-year price of a typical cottage, condominium or chalet was up between 9 and 10 per cent.

Businesses that rely on a strong housing market also had a good year. Canadians who gussied up their homes and laboured on summer renovation projects helped power Rona Inc. to its best quarterly performance ever, doubling the home-improvement company's profit in the second quarter of 2004 compared with a year earlier.

Rona and its competitors— Canadian Tire Corp., Home Depot and Home Hardware Stores—also benefited from social and economic factors such as the effects of an aging population and aging houses. Analysts said today's seniors were healthy enough to renovate their own homes and keep their gardens in top condition, and could spend lots of time at home-improvement stores.

Over 60,000 fans crowd Edmonton's Commonwealth Stadium for an outdoor hockey game between the Edmonton Oilers and Montreal Canadiens. (Jeff McIntosh/CP)

PART 5
Sports

THE NEW

Wayne Gretzky watches play from the blue-line during outdoor alumni game. (Adrian Wyld/CP)

Hockey fans bundle up for unique outdoor doubleheader in Edmonton

Marketing whizzes dreamed up the slogan "Hockey in the Heartland" to promote a National Hockey League game played outdoors. But the fans who sat in arctic temperatures for up to eight hours on November 22, 2003, earned the rights to the name.

Never mind that it was -16 C for the Heritage Classic match-up between the megastars—former Edmonton Oiler greats and the alumni of the legendary Montreal

Canadiens. Never mind that the mercury plunged even further, to a punishing -20 C, during the contest between the current Oilers and Canadiens in the first-ever NHL game played outdoors.

Nearly 58,000 bundled-up, hockey-obsessed fans packed the Commonwealth Stadium to watch the doubleheader, and tens of thousands were still there for the fireworks after the games. "These are people that

Former Oilers Mark Messier, left, and Ken Linseman take a break during outdoor exhibition game. (Adrian Wyld/CP)

didn't have access to tents or boxes to get warm; they braved the cold, but that's what Edmontonians are all about," said Mayor Bill Smith. Out-of-town visitors from as far away as Toronto, Ottawa and, of course, Montreal shared some of the credit.

"I don't care if I freeze my butt off, it's worth every minute of it," said Janelle Conn of Beaumont, Alta. Conn was wrapped in a sleeping bag and wore battery-operated socks, leotards, long johns, jeans, a ski jacket and mittens.

The success of the event may have given other NHL teams ideas, but it was an event that will be hard to duplicate. Wayne Gretzky played his one-and-only old-timers' game. His 14-year-old daughter sang "I Will Remember You" as giant video screens showed replays of the icon of the City of Champions playing shinny in a toque. There was a jet flyover, a streaker, a snowball fight and an Oilers attack in the final minutes that decided the game. The alumni game ended 2-0 for Gretzky and Company, while Montreal won the regulation game 4-3.

Players in both games went home thrilled. "Oh my God, I was freezing," Montreal forward Richard Zednik said. "It was fun, though." Gretzky called the experience "magical" while Canadiens great Guy Lafleur joked, "If the NHL goes on strike, we'll come back."

Former Oiler Paul Coffey and former Canadien Guy Lafleur laugh while watching a streaker at the alumni game. (Adrian Wyld/CP)

ATHENS 2004

Lori-Ann Muenzer of Edmonton celebrates her gold medal win for sprint cycling. (Adrian Wyld/CP)

Opposite page from top to bottom
Émilie Heymans, left, and Blythe Hartley, Adam van Koeverden, Alexandre Despatie, Marie-Hélène Prémont, Chantal Petitclerc

(Tom Hanson/CP)

(Adrian Wyld/CP)

(Adrian Wyld/CP)

(Paul Chiasson/CP)

(Mike Ridewood/CP/COC)

High hopes—little gold

Canada's Olympic team went to the 2004 Summer Games in Athens hoping to at least match the 14 medals it won in Sydney in 2000. But the final Athens total of 12 medals (three gold, six silver and three bronze) is the fewest Canada has won since 1988 in Seoul.

Four medals thought to be locks—Perdita Felicien in the 100-metre hurdles, Alexandre Despatie and Émilie Heymans in the 10-metre platform diving, the men's eight rowers—never came through. Although these failures were disappointing, there were some other historical Canadian finishes to cheer:

- Kayaker Adam van Koeverden won gold in the men's single 500 metres and bronze in the 1,000 metres, the first time Canada had won a medal in either event. The 22-year-old from Oakville, Ont., also became the first Canadian athlete to win more than one medal at a Summer Olympics since 1996.
- Lori-Ann Muenzer of Edmonton earned Canada's first ever gold medal in cycling when the 38-year-old won the track sprint event.
- Kyle Shewfelt of Calgary became the first Canadian to win an artistic gymnastics medal when he took the gold in the floor exercise.
- Ross Macdonald of Vancouver and Mike Wolfs of Port Credit, Ont., won silver for Canada's first sailing medal in 12 years.
- With her silver, Tonya Verbeek of Beamsville, Ont., was the first Canadian woman to win a wrestling medal.
- Caroline Brunet of Lac-Beauport, Que., won a kayak bronze, coming home with a medal for the third consecutive Games (after silver in both 1996 and 2000). That matched the consecutive medal streaks of Lesley Thompson (rowing) and Phil Edwards (athletics).

▲ Chantal Petitclerc of Montreal wins gold in the women's 800-metre wheelchair race. (Tom Hanson/CP)

Still, the image most Canadians will remember from Athens is a dejected Felicien slumped against a fallen hurdle after crashing just 13 metres into her race. Her misery had plenty of company. The swim team failed to win a medal for the first time in 40 years. And the track team missed getting a medal for the second Olympics in a row. Heymans and Despatie disappointed in the 10-metre platform, where they are both world champions. The rowing team won just one medal instead of the three to five they had predicted.

Coming into the Games, Canada had 34 athletes, teams or crews ranked in the top five in the world in 2003. Only nine won medals. None of Canada's four world champions even made it to the podium in their event.

The medal numbers prompted much discussion on what could– or should–be done to improve Canada's showing at the international sporting event, with many suggesting more funding was needed. The federal government said it would look at what has been done in other countries, such as Australia, that have seen their athletes on the Olympic podium time and again. Canada is the only nation to host an Olympics and not win a gold medal on two occasions—at the 1976 Summer Olympics in Montreal and the 1988 Winter Games in Calgary. (Jim Morris, CP)

Clockwise from top: Perdita Felicien falls in hurdles (Julie Jacobson/AP); Adam Kreek, left, and Andrew Hoskins cross the finish line in the men's eight rowing (Paul Chiasson/CP); Karen Cockburn receives silver medal in trampoline (Kevork Djansezian/AP); Nicolas Gill throws Italy's Michele Monti, left, in judo (Ryan Remiorz/CP); Kyle Shewfelt competes in the floor exercise in gymnastics (Nhat V. Meyer/AP). ▶

Canada loses heartbreaker to United States at World Junior Hockey Championship

There was only heartbreak in Helsinki for Canada's junior hockey team in January 2004. Canada settled for silver for the third consecutive year at the world junior championships as the United States scored three un-answered goals in the third period to defeat the Canadians 4-3 and capture its first junior title. The loss pushed Canada's gold medal drought at the under-20 championship to seven years, although it remained the only country to win a medal in six straight tournaments with four silver and two bronze.

Goaltender Marc-Andre Fleury of the Pittsburgh Penguins, last year's tournament MVP, had a nightmarish ending to the final, giving up the winning goal with 5:12 remaining when his attempt to clear the puck bounced off a Canadian defenceman into his own net. "It wasn't his fault. It was just a bad bounce," said Canadian captain Dan Paille. (Donna Spencer, CP)

◀ Ryan Getzlaf after medal presentation at the world junior championship. (Adrian Wyld/CP)

Lennox Lewis becomes first heavyweight boxing champ to retire since Rocky Marciano

A boxing career that began in a Kitchener, Ont., police gym without a proper ring ended in London, England, when Lennox Lewis, the reigning world heavyweight champion, announced his retirement.

With six championship belts draped on a podium around him, Lewis said he fought his final bout in Los Angeles in June 2003 when he beat Vitali Klitschko and announced he wouldn't defend his World Boxing Council title in a rematch against the Ukrainian. "I realize that this is the drug of the sport; there's always one more fight, always somebody to fight," Lewis, 38, told a packed news conference on February 6, 2004. "I don't really want to get caught up in it. There has to be a time when I should gracefully bow out."

Lewis's decision made him the first reigning heavyweight champion to retire since Rocky Marciano in 1956, and only the third in history to leave at the top. His professional record is an impressive 41-1-2, with victories over the best heavyweights of his time, including Mike Tyson and Evander Holyfield. As an amateur he won a gold medal for Canada at the 1988 Olympics in Seoul.

Born in London but raised in Kitchener, Ont., Lewis began boxing after a school principal suggested it as an alternative to schoolyard fights as a way of settling scores with kids who teased him over his East London accent.

There's no chance of a comeback, Lewis told reporters in London, where he moved to conduct his pro career. "I have always asked myself the question of why old heavyweights come back and I plan to stay out of the ring." (Kevin Ward, CP)

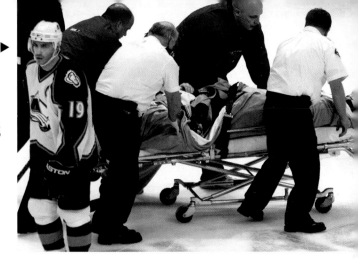

Ugly incident on ice causes serious injuries to hockey player and another black eye for the NHL

Todd Bertuzzi of the Vancouver Canucks plays hockey like a big kid. He'll whack a teammate with his stick or bounce a puck off their leg, then look at them with a big gap-toothed grin. At six-foot-three and 245 pounds, he's been described as the perfect hockey player, from the neck down. He's the Canucks' highest-paid player at almost US$7 million a season.

There are times, though, when the child takes over the man. Bertuzzi can be surly and sometimes is a bully. He often takes stupid penalties. It's this mixture of hockey talent combined with unpredictable emotions that led to a shocking incident on March 9, 2004, that prompted one of the most talked-about hockey stories of the year.

It was a home game and the Canucks were losing, badly, to the Colorado Avalanche. In the third period, Bertuzzi charged up the ice, grabbed the sweater of rookie Steve Moore of the Avalanche from behind, then slugged him with a wild, round-house punch. The two players fell, with Bertuzzi landing on top of Moore, ramming his face into the ice. A pool of blood formed around Moore's head. Medical staff rushed onto the ice, strapped him onto a stretcher and rushed him to hospital. He had three fractured vertebrae, facial cuts, significant post-concussion symptoms and "significant amnesia." Nerves in the neck area were stretched by the blow.

The incident also ended Bertuzzi's season, thanks to a suspension that included the playoffs, and he must apply to the league for reinstatement. He was fined more than $500,000 and eventually charged by police with assault. The ugly incident was another black eye for the NHL, coming on the heels of a brawl-filled game between the Ottawa Senators and Philadelphia Flyers that set an NHL record of 419 penalty minutes. It didn't help that the Bertuzzi bloodbath also tarnished the NHL trade deadline day—normally a dream day for hockey junkies.

Bertuzzi made a tearful public apology to Moore. "I had no intention of hurting you," he said. "I feel awful for what transpired. I don't play the game that way. I'm not a mean-spirited person."

Moore did not pass much comment publicly on Bertuzzi's actions, except to say "that kind of stuff doesn't have any place in the game." But many NHL players called it a cheap shot. Some applauded the suspension handed to Bertuzzi but doubted it would deter further violence on the ice. Others said that no matter how severe the punishment, it is in the nature of a fast, physical sport that players will sometimes lose their tempers and that a split-second of madness is all it takes to produce a serious injury. (Jim Morris, Bill Beacon, Shi Davidi, CP)

Led by Clara Hughes, Canadians win big at world speed skating

Clara Hughes of Glen Sutton, Que., is an unusual athlete, the only Canadian who has won a medal at both the Summer and Winter Olympic Games. She started as a cyclist, winning two bronze medals in Atlanta in 1996, then switched to speed skating, winning a bronze in Salt Lake City in 2002. The speed skating success continued in 2004, when she won her first world title, a gold medal in the women's 5,000 metres at the long-track speed-skating world single-distance championships in Seoul.

"This is probably my biggest thrill after my Olympic medals," Hughes said. "With two laps to go I was hurting so much. It was then that I needed to make a decision. And I decided to fight. I skated the race of my life and exhausted everything I had."

Hughes's gold medal capped a strong performance by Canadian long-track speed skaters in South Korea. Jeremy Wotherspoon of Red Deer, Alta., added silver in the men's 1,000 to end a superb season. Cindy Klassen of Winnipeg took bronze in the women's 1,000. Canada ended the competition with six medals—two gold, two silver and two bronze.

▲ Clara Hughes skates her way to winning the ladies' 5000-meter event at the 2004 world single-distance speed-skating championships in Seoul. (Yun Jai-hyoung/AP)

Emanuel Sandhu performs his long program at the 2004 world figure skating championships. (Paul Chiasson/CP)

A 22-year streak of world figure skating championship medals is broken

For the first time in 23 years, there were no medals for Canada at the world figure skating championships, held in Dortmund, Germany, in 2004. The unlikely star of Canada's team turned out to be Joannie Rochette, an 18-year-old Quebecer who zoomed all the way to eighth place from 17th the year before.

Canadian men's champion Emanuel Sandhu of Richmond Hill, Ont., finished eighth, the same spot as a year earlier, after Evgeni Plushenko of Russia won with one of the most technically fantastic performances in any free-skating final. Sandhu, in 11th place after an awful short program, was strong enough in the long skate to move up three spots. "I said to myself, 'I can't change anything right now and I don't want to go out wimpy,'" he said. "I wanted to go out fighting. It's hard to recover from something like that, especially when you're starting out hoping to win a medal and you know you've blown it."

Canada's woman champion, Jennifer Robinson of Windsor, Ont., a veteran of eight world figure skating championships, announced her retirement after a 14th-place showing, down five spots from the previous year. (Neil Stevens, CP)

▲ Therese Brisson, Colleen Sostorics, Delaney Collins, Dana Antal and Cherie Piper celebrate their win. (Andrew Vaughan/CP)

Canadian women's hockey team wins eighth world title

Canada's reign continued at the women's world hockey championship in 2004, with a 2-0 win over the United States before a deafening, sellout crowd in Halifax. Hayley Wickenheiser and Delaney Collins scored for Canada, which has won all eight women's titles since the tournament began in 1990.

"It's not easy at all to go out there and play in front of these kinds of crowds and there's the pressure to continue [the streak]," said Wickenheiser. "This team just finds a way to do it all the time."

The tournament confirmed that, outside of North America, women's hockey is still barely out of its infancy. Canada and the United States, who have met in every final, continued to be far out in front of the rest of the field.

After the game, Canadian captain Cassie Campbell clutched the new silver cup. Her voice cracked and she smelled of champagne after a few celebratory soakings in the dressing room. "Eight championships in a row and some of those games have gone into overtime. It's just incredible," she said.

Finland edged Sweden 3-2 for the bronze at the Halifax championships, which set an attendance record of 94,000 fans. (Donna Spencer, CP)

Calgary Flames: Cinderella team becomes Stanley Cup contender

In Calgary, it became known as the Red Mile—a trippy strip of ethnic eateries, fast-food huts and knick-knack shops south of downtown punctuated at its easternmost point by the signature double-curved roof of the Saddledome. The stretch of 17th Avenue SW was informally renamed in honour of the city's beloved red and gold Calgary Flames.

Fans garbed in the colours of their hockey heroes went wild almost nightly during the 2004 Stanley Cup playoffs as their Flames torched 15 years of misery by out-hustling and out-muscling three division champs—the Vancouver Canucks, Detroit Red Wings and San Jose Sharks—only to be finally stopped by the Tampa Bay Lightning in Game 7 of the Cup Final.

It was the latest chapter in a thrilling story that began 32 years ago in the Deep South of the United States. The Flames were born in Atlanta as part of the National Hockey League's rapid expansion in the late 1960s and early '70s. Named for the burning of the city during the U.S. Civil War, the team took to the ice on October 7, 1972, and burned brightly in the early days. But as the seasons passed, fans in Dixie began to look away. Players' salaries blew the budget for team owner Tom Cousins, TV ratings floundered and the team endured five straight first-round playoff losses.

A group led by Vancouver businessman Nelson Skalbania bought the team in 1980 and brought

◀ Flames fans pack the streets of Calgary after their team's victory in the third game of the Stanley Cup Final. (Jeff McIntosh/CP)

the Flames north to open arms and an ancient rink—the Calgary Corral. The name and the red and gold jerseys stayed, with the fiery A becoming the flaming C. On October 9, 1980, the Quebec Nordiques came to town for the Flames' first regular-season NHL game.

During the 1980s the Flames went on a roller-coaster ride to the top. With coaches Bob Johnson and later Terry Crisp, and star players Doug Gilmour, Lanny McDonald, Joe Nieuwendyk and goalie Mike Vernon, the Flames joined the league's elite but found it tough to match the benchmark set a three-hour drive north, where Wayne Gretzky and the Edmonton Oilers had fashioned a dynasty.

There were successes, notably in 1986 when they beat the hated Oilers in the second round of the playoffs. The victory proved pyrrhic—the Flames lost their first Stanley Cup final that year to the Montreal Canadiens. Three years later, the Flames put it all together, roaring through the regular season as the league's top

point-getter and flattening all comers in the playoffs to win the Stanley Cup over the Canadiens.

The Flames' time on the summit of Mount Stanley was short and their subsequent fall in the 1990s was swift and steep. They lost in the first round in six of the next seven years and, starting in 1997, missed the playoffs altogether until 2004.

The seeds for success were there in the form of star right-winger Jarome Iginla, but nothing took root until Christmas 2002, when Darryl Sutter, recently fired as coach of the San Jose Sharks, was hired as the new bench boss. The team missed the playoffs in Sutter's first year, but as 2003-04 began, the stated goal was to make the post-season and take it from there.

The key was Iginla. The 26-year-old captain, an Olympic gold medal winner and former NHL scoring leader with a hard shot and soft hands, was looking to justify his king's ransom salary of US$7.5 million. He started slowly but excelled down the stretch to tie

▼ Ruslan Fedotenko of Tampa Bay gets a goal past Miikka Kiprusoff of the Flames in Game 7 of the Stanley Cup Final. (Ryan Remiorz/CP)

for the league lead with 41 goals.

The final piece of the puzzle was Finnish goaltender Miikka Kiprusoff, added after Flames net-minder Roman Turek went down with a knee injury in November. Kiprusoff was 27, with a whip-fast glove hand and a hunger to prove himself.

The team finished with 94 points, good for sixth place in the Western Conference. The stage was set for the amazing playoff run that electrified the southern Alberta oil centre. The red jersey with the black flaming C became the new unofficial uniform for school and the attire for work. The red C flew from car flags, was painted onto buildings and on top of lawns. Strippers in clubs cut their acts short on game night rather than compete with the play-by-play action on TV.

As the four other Canadian teams faded from the playoff picture, Calgary's team became Canada's. The joyous epicentre was still the Red Mile, where tens of thousands spilled from bars after games to high-five and hug, to stand on, ride in, or hang precariously from cars roaring down roads, honking horns into the wee hours.

▲ Captain Dave Andreychuk of Tampa Bay raises the Stanley Cup in victory after Game 7 on June 7. (Ryan Remiorz/CP)

It was a great ride that lasted as long as it could—until the seventh game of the final series in Tampa Bay, when the Flames lost a 2-1 heartbreaker to the Lightning, denying them the Cup but giving them the consolation prize of being the first Canadian team in a decade to make it that far.

"It's the toughest loss by a thousand times," said Iginla. "One shot. The guys worked so hard. It's a very good season and I'm so proud of everybody but that hurts more than anything else I've been a part of." (Dean Bennett, CP)

Brad Richards and the Stanley Cup ▶ parade through Murray Harbour, P.E.I. on a lobster boat. (Brian McInnis/*Charlottetown Guardian*)

The Stanley Cup comes to P.E.I.

There was one corner of Canada that looked at the Stanley Cup final as a win. Brad Richards, star centre for the Tampa Bay Lightning and the pride of Murray Harbour, P.E.I., had a huge contingent of followers on the Island who saw the final in terms of the Flames versus Brad—an all-Canadian contest.

A league tradition allows each member of the winning team to borrow the Cup for a day. When Richards showed up in Murray Harbour with it, more than 10,000 people flooded the tiny, rural community to get a glimpse. "Besides winning [the Cup] that night and lifting it on the ice, this is definitely the best day of my life," Richardson, whose parents are in the lobster fishing business, told reporters. The Cup, displayed on the bow of a fishing boat named the *Murray Harbour*, was towed in a parade along the main street, then put on display along with Richards' other trophies—the Lady Byng trophy as the NHL's most sportsman-like player and the Conn Smythe as playoff's MVP—at a ball field.

Canada's first major league baseball club fades away

For those who watched the Montreal Expos play their final game at the Big-O, it was hard to imagine they were once the toast of the city and a point of pride for all of Canada.

When they became Canada's first Major League Baseball club in 1969, with Rusty (Le Grand Orange) Staub as their star outfielder, or when a supremely gifted young team fell to the Los Angeles Dodgers in the National League Championship Series in 1981, the Expos were hot.

But memories seemed to be all that was left in 2004 as baseball negotiated the transfer of the once-thriving franchise to Washington, D.C., for 2005. It was a sad phenomenon for the team that once drew more than 2 million fans a year to cavernous Olympic Stadium.

Three factors killed the Expos: the loss of a deep-pocketed owner after Charles Bronfman sold the club in 1991; a weak Canadian dollar in an era of skyrocketing player salaries; and a players strike in 1994 that wiped out their best chance to reach the World Series.

It was not how it was supposed to turn out when it all started in giddy anticipation in 1967, when city councillor Gerry Snyder presented a bid for an expansion franchise to National League owners. The next year, after Bronfman saved the bid by moving in as the lead owner, Montreal became the first non-U.S. club in the majors. The big day finally came on April 8, 1969, when the Expos, named for the city's hugely successful world's fair called Expo 67, won their inaugural game 11-10 against the Mets in New York. But the love affair really began with their home opener at the patched-together stadium at Jarry Park on April 14, an 8-7 win over the St. Louis Cardinals before a sellout crowd of 29,184.

It was a different story by 2004, however. Only 3,923 fans were on hand for the opener of the team's final series in Montreal. "It's a little disheartening," Expos reliever Joey Eischen said. "You'd like to think it might mean a little more to the people." (Bill Beacon, CP)

◀ The Expos bid adieu to their Montreal fans on September 29, 2004. (Ryan Remiorz/CP)

Beckie Scott: Olympic champion at last

It was described as the longest race in Olympic history. On June 25, 2004, Canadian cross-country skier Beckie Scott finally received the gold medal for the five-km pursuit race at the 2002 Winter Games. Scott also went into the record books for being the only Olympic athlete to be awarded all three medals in a single event.

Scott initially won the bronze medal at the Games in Salt Lake City, but then waited over two years as first the silver medallist and then the gold medallist, both Russians, were stripped of their medals for failing drug tests.

The gold medal ceremony was the most emotional for the 29-year-old from Vermilion, Alta. More than 500 people gathered outside the Vancouver Art Gallery to watch Scott flash a broad smile and choke back tears as *O Canada* was sung and a Mountie hoisted a Maple Leaf up a flag pole. "It's a fantastic day, a great day," said Scott. "I'm in some ways still in disbelief it's actually here." (Jim Morris, CP)

▼ Beckie Scott displays her gold medal in Vancouver. (Chris Bolin/CP)

▲ From left, Colleen Jones, Kim Kelly, Mary-Anne Arsenault and Nancy Delahunt display their curling hardware. (Andrew Vaughan/CP)

Canadian women strike gold among the rocks at world curling championships

The pride was as plain as the Maple Leaf on Colleen Jones's back after she claimed her second women's world curling title at the championships in Gavle, Sweden, in April 2004. "It's something you dream of ever since you were a little kid and then it's something you dream about through the season that you might get the opportunity to do," said Jones.

With six Canadian championships and two world titles, Jones and her Halifax team of Kim Kelly, Mary-Anne Arsenault and Nancy Delahunt were not resting on their laurels after the win, but looking for a new challenge to keep them going for another few seasons. Jones had no problems coming up with one. "An Olympic gold," she said.

Canada's men didn't enjoy the same success in Sweden. Mark Dacey and his rink, also from Halifax, fell to Germany in the semifinals, which put them in the bronze medal game. This they won handily, crushing Olympic gold medallist Pal Trulsen and his Norway rink 9-3. (Bill Graveland, CP)

World champions put Canada at forefront of sliding sports

Former Olympic champion Pierre Lueders and skeleton racer Duff Gibson took gold medals at the world championships in Germany in 2004, a strong reminder that Canada is at the forefront of competitors in the sliding sports, despite only nodding interest from the Canadian public.

For Gibson, a 37-year-old firefighter, the world title was his first international win after five years in the sport. Despite his advanced age—in athletic terms—Gibson says he's nowhere near finished. "That time seems to be going later and later," Gibson said. "You see that in the sprinting world with world records being set by athletes well into their 30s. I'm still getting better every year."

Sliding sports require strong driving skills that can take years to develop, meaning that it's rare to see people in their early 20s taking medals in luge or skeleton, where athletes aim headfirst down the track protected by just a helmet.

After three straight second-place finishes, Lueders finally ended his world championship jinx, capturing his first-ever world title in the two-man bobsled. "I thought that maybe I'll always be known as the guy that finished in second place, that I was the guy that would never win a world championship but would always have five or six silvers," the Edmonton native said. The 33-year-old Lueders and brakeman Giulio Zardo of Montreal edged German Olympic champion Christoph Langen by .22 seconds on his home track.

Pierre Lueders, front, and brakeman Giulio Zardo win the world title in the two-man bobsled in Lake Placid, N.Y. (Todd Bissonette/AP)

▲ Smarty Jones and jockey Stewart Elliott cross the finish line at the Kentucky Derby on May 1, 2004. (Al Behrman/AP)

Toronto-born jockey rides horse racing sensation of the year

The horse-racing sensation of the year was an undersized three-year-old named Smarty Jones. And it was a Toronto-born jockey who guided Smarty to within a whisker of being the first Triple Crown winner since 1978.

Stewart Elliott, 39, gained international prominence in 2004 by guiding Smarty to victory in the Kentucky Derby and the Preakness Stakes. They lost in the Belmont, denying Smarty the opportunity of becoming only the 12th horse in racing history to win the Triple Crown.

"The first week [after Belmont] was tough, but now I look back on it we had a great run," said Elliott. "He actually ran a faster mile and a quarter in the Belmont than he did when he won the Kentucky Derby, so what can you say?"

Elliott, born in Toronto, grew up around horses—his father was a jockey and his mother rode show horses. He began riding professionally at age 16. On May 1, 2004, he became the first jockey in 25 years to win the Kentucky Derby in his first appearance in the race.

In 2004 he also finally realized his dream of riding in the $1-million Queen's Plate, Canada's most prestigious thoroughbred race, at Woodbine Racetrack in Toronto. The race, however, was a huge disappointment. His horse—Long Pond, owned by pharmaceutical mogul Eugene Melnyk—came in dead last.

Marlene Stewart Streit is first Canadian to join World Golf Hall of Fame

The only golfer to have won the Canadian, Australian, British and American women's amateur championships is Marlene Stewart Streit. She was also the first Canadian to be admitted to the World Golf Hall of Fame in St. Augustine, Florida, in 2004.

"I played golf all my life for the love of the game," Streit, 70, said after hearing the news. "This is very huge for Canada, and I'm just proud. My greatest thrill in golf has been playing for my country."

Streit, who was selected in the veterans' category, won eleven Canadian Ladies Open Amateur titles, nine Canadian Ladies Close Amateur titles and three Canadian Senior Women's Amateur tournaments. She has also won four USGA events, including the 1956 U.S. Women's Amateur. In 2003, she captured her third U.S. Senior Women's Amateur, becoming the oldest person to ever win the tournament. The native of Unionville, Ont., was chosen as *The Canadian Press* female Athlete of the Year five times in the 1950s and '60s.

She never turned pro because the prize money for women was not much of a lure when she was starting out in the 1950s, and when she graduated from university she chose to raise a family while entering selected tournaments. "I don't look back and say, 'Gosh, if I'd turned pro, what would I have done?'" she once commented. "I know what I would have done. I would have been great out there."

◀ Marlene Stewart Streit swings her clubs in Stouffville, Ont., in 1999. (Rene Johnston/CP)

Golfer Stephen Ames, left, smiles after winning Western Open in Lemont, Ill., while Mike Weir has a different reaction after missing a putt on the 18th hole of the final round of the Canadian Open in Oakville, Ont. (Jeff Roberson/AP, Frank Gunn/CP)

Disappointment for Weir, but Ames records first PGA win

There was heartbreak at the Glen Abbey golf course in Oakville, Ont., as hometown hero Mike Weir failed to become the first Canadian in 50 years to win the Bell Canadian Open. Weir, who won the Nissan Open and made more than US$2.5 million on the PGA Tour in 2004, led for much of the tournament but had to settle for second after losing to world-ranked No. 1 Vijay Singh on a third-hole playoff.

Weir's fellow Canadian on the PGA Tour, Stephen Ames made headlines when he shot a 70 to win the Western Open in Lemont, Ill.—his first PGA triumph. The victory was a long time coming. Ames, who was born in Trinidad and became a Canadian citizen in 2003, had been playing as a pro since 1987 and joined the PGA Tour in 1996. It was a breakout year for Ames, who came home to the Canadian Open with some US$3 million in money winnings for the season.

NHL hockey star charged in friend and teammate's death in car crash

Dany Heatley, left, leaves funeral of teammate Dan Snyder in Elmira, Ont. (Tobin Grimshaw/CP)

A terrible car crash that killed his friend and teammate Dan Snyder continues to have reverberations for Dany Heatley of the NHL's Atlanta Thrashers in 2004.

Heatley, 23, who was driving his black 2002 Ferrari convertible at a high rate of speed when it ran into a brick pillar and iron fence outside a condominium in Atlanta on September 29, 2003, was indicted on vehicular homicide and five other charges. Snyder, a 25-year-old from Elmira, Ont., was the sole passenger.

The road's speed limit was 56 km an hour. Fulton County District Attorney Paul Howard estimated Heatley's car was travelling as fast as 130 km/h.

After the crash, Heatley spent time with Snyder's family and attended a Dan Snyder memorial golf tournament. The Snyder family said they did not blame Heatley for Snyder's death. "Our feelings have never changed and we continue to support Dany and the entire Heatley family," the family said after the charges were announced. "Despite our personal feelings in this matter, we respect the responsibility of the district attorney's office and the legal process."

After missing over half of the season recovering from his injuries, Heatley returned to the Thrashers in January 2004 and then led Canada to a world hockey championship gold medal in Prague in May. He also played for Canada in the World Cup of Hockey in September 2004.

▼ Dany Heatley's car, a 2002 Ferrari 360 Modena, after the crash that killed his teammate Dan Snyder. (Ben Gray/*Atlanta Journal-Constitution*)

Determined Team Canada comes from behind to take men's world hockey title

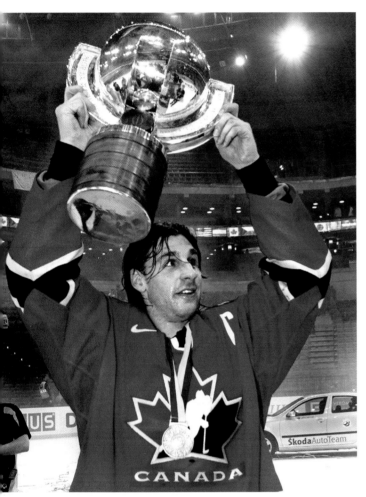

▲ Captain Ryan Smyth holds the championship cup for world hockey. (Chuck Stoody/CP)

The swagger came back to Canadian hockey in April 2004 when a determined Team Canada came from behind for the third straight game to capture a second straight men's world hockey championship, with a thrilling 5-3 win over Sweden in Prague.

Six years after hosting a summit to fix what was wrong with the national pastime, all indications were that Canada was back where it belonged. "Yeah, I think we can put that to rest now," said champagne-soaked forward Brenden Morrow after the win. "We proved that hockey is Canada's game again."

At the start of the tournament, few would have believed another gold medal was on its way. The team was rocked on the eve of its first game with the loss of head coach Joel Quenneville after he fell ill. Canada, assembled by general manager Jim Nill, opened with a 2-2 tie to lowly Austria, barely beat France 3-0 and was later crushed 6-2 by the Czech Republic in the final round-robin game. But then came a 5-4 quarter-final win over Finland and a 2-1 semifinal victory over talented Slovakia, both come-from-behind victories.

It was the first time Canada had captured back-to-back world championships since the Whitby Dunlops (1958) and Belleville McFarlands (1959) turned the trick nearly half a century ago. (Pierre LeBrun, CP)

From left, Mike Ilitch, Pat LaFontaine, Grant Fuhr and Brian Kilrea ▶
pose after being presented with their jackets and rings at the
Hockey Hall of Fame in Toronto in November 2003. (Frank Gunn/CP)

Shane Doan of Team Canada scores past Miikka Kiprusoff of Team Finland during the World Cup of Hockey final in Toronto. (Adrian Wyld/CP)

▲ Team Canada captain Mario Lemieux holds the championship trophy. (Ryan Remiorz/CP)

Canada grabs another international hockey title

Team Canada romped through the 2004 World Cup of Hockey, an eight-country tournament staged jointly by the National Hockey League and the NHL Players' Association.

Wayne Gretzky resumed his role as executive director of Team Canada and selected a youthful and skilled lineup that never once trailed in a game en route to a perfect 6-0-0 record and a 3-2 win over surprise finalist Finland in the championship game at Air Canada Centre in Toronto on September 14.

Canada's biggest test came in the semifinals when the Czech Republic forced overtime with a late goal, but Vincent Lecavalier scored in extra time to give the Canadians a 4-3 win. Lecavalier was later named tournament MVP.

It was the first time the World Cup, formerly the Canada Cup, had been held in eight years. Canada won the tournament for the fifth time in seven tries. (Pierre LeBrun, CP)

◀ Clockwise from top: Team Canada members gather around executive director Wayne Gretzky. (Frank Gunn/CP)

Hockey fans take to the streets of Toronto to celebrate Team Canada's victory over Finland. (J.P. Moczulski/CP)

Team Canada goaltender Martin Brodeur celebrates the victory. (Ryan Remiorz/CP)

NHL
awards

Clockwise from top: New Jersey Devils goalie Martin Brodeur with his sons William (right) and Jeremy at the annual NHL awards in Toronto. Brodeur won the Vezina trophy for best goaltending, and shared the William Jennings trophy for the team with the fewest goals scored against. (Adrian Wyld/CP)

Calgary Flames Jarome Iginla poses with the Maurice Richard trophy, for top goal-scorer, and the King Clancy humanitarian trophy. (Adrian Wyld/CP)

Martin St-Louis of the Tampa Bay Lightning with his Lester B. Pearson trophy, given to the player voted MVP by his peers. (Derek Oliver/CP)

PART 6

Crime and Punishment

Brutal murders of little girls shock Toronto

Farah Khan. Cecilia Zhang. Holly Jones. The faces of three little girls, all the victims of brutal murders, haunted the thoughts of Torontonians in 2004.

Five-year-old Farah, barely three feet tall and weighing 35 pounds, was savagely beaten to death by her father while her stepmother watched. Muhammad Arsal Khan chopped up her body and scattered pieces around Toronto parks in December 1999. He was convicted of first-degree murder and sentenced to life without parole for at least 25 years for a crime that had even a city somewhat inured to violence gasping in revulsion. His wife, Kaneez Fatima, was convicted of second-degree murder and ordered to spend at least 15 years behind bars.

Nine-year-old Cecilia was taken from her bed in her family's Toronto home in a daring abduction that initially left police baffled and pulled at the heartstrings of Canada's most populous city. For months her whereabouts was a mystery. Then her skeletal remains were discovered in March 2004 in a wooded area behind a church in the city of Mississauga, west of Toronto. A few months later police charged 21-year-old Min Chen, in Canada on a student visa, with her murder.

◀ Sherry Xu, left, and Raymond Zhang bow at the end of a memorial service for their daughter Cecilia Zhang at the Peoples Church of Toronto. (Aaron Harris/CP)

Ten-year-old Holly vanished off a west-end street while she was walking home in the early evening from a friend's house in May 2003. Michael Briere, a software programmer who lived a few blocks from Holly, pleaded guilty to her murder more than a year later, after he was linked to her death by DNA evidence. Briere had grabbed her off the street, sexually assaulted her in his nearby apartment, then killed and dismembered her. He claimed he was acting out his fantasy to have sex with a child after being spurred on by Internet pornography. Briere received an automatic life sentence with no parole eligibility for 25 years.

Together, the three cases seemed to suggest a frightening rise in random and deadly violence in the country. Statistics showed otherwise, although it was hard to persuade people haunted by these girls'

▲ Nine-year-old Cecilia Zhang.
(Toronto Police/CP)

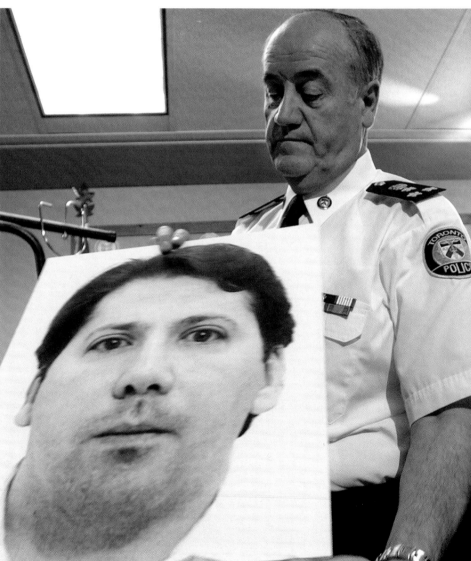

Chief Julian Fantino of Toronto police ▶
holds a photograph of Michael Brier,
who pleaded guilty to the murder of
Holly Jones. (J.P. Moczulski/CP)

Three mothers mourn. Above: Maria Jones, mother of Holly. (Kevin Frayer/CP) Top left: Sherry Xu, left, mother of Cecilia Zhang, with her daughter's best friend Gloria. (Aaron Harris/CP) Bottom left: Shahida Jabeen, mother of Farah Khan. (Tannis Toohey/*Toronto Star*)

young faces. In 2003, Canada's murder rate dropped to lows not seen since 1967, with a total of 548 homicides reported across the country, 34 fewer than in 2002. Toronto had the third-lowest crime rate in the Statistics Canada study

"The overall picture of crime in Canada looks very much like it looked last year and the year before that and the year before that," said criminologist Rosemary Gartner of the University of Toronto. "It does not support claims by some people or concerns expressed by some that Canada is becoming a more violent place."

Repeated media reports of high-profile tragedies such as a child abduction sometimes give the false impression violent crime is rampant, she said. "It's the rarest and most unusual forms of crime that tend to drive people's fears the most."

Crime and Punishment |

▲ Svend Robinson, right, with his partner Max Riveron, tells a news conference he stole a diamond ring. (Chuck Stoody/CP)

"Shattered" former MP Svend Robinson given conditional discharge for stealing ring

He suffered intense humiliation and was shamed out of public office and that was punishment enough, the judge said. Svend Robinson, one of Canada's best-known MPs, walked out of court without jail time or a criminal conviction in August 2004 after pleading guilty to stealing a diamond ring.

"In Canada, we don't kick people when they're down," said Judge Ron Fratkin, who gave Robinson a conditional discharge and sentenced him to 100 hours of community service. He added that Robinson "has fallen far further than most, all for a bauble, a trinket, a ring."

Robinson, re-elected seven times as an MP, had been sliding towards a breakdown, Fratkin noted, and people close to him could see it coming. "His lawyers say it was a one-off, a result of pressure that was somewhat self-imposed and pressure brought on by others seeking his help," Fratkin said.

Court was told that Robinson had gone to a public auction over the Easter long weekend in April. He had been shopping for a diamond ring for his partner, Max Riveron, earlier in the week, and looked at rings at the auction. He pocketed one, valued at a retail price of $21,500, then took it out to his car and hid it. Then he returned to the auction and continued to browse.

A few days later, Robinson, 52, admitted his guilt during a televised news conference, and later announced he would step aside from his duties as an MP to take medical leave. He did not run in the June election.

Robinson, looking gaunt and nervous, pleaded guilty to theft over $5,000. "This has been a shattering experience for me," Robinson told the court. "I feel remorse and shame for a totally unthinkable act." (Amy Carmichael, CP)

Judge sentenced for sexually assaulting young prostitutes who appeared in his court

The young prostitutes working the streets of Prince George, B.C., said everyone had been familiar with provincial court judge David Ramsay for years.

Ramsay had a reputation for promising big money for sex. He liked young girls and would drive them into the woods, force himself on them and then kick them, naked, out of his truck without paying.

Ramsay, 61, was sentenced in June 2004 to seven years in prison after he admitted to sex-related charges against four females, one as young as 12. It was a severe punishment that rocked the legal community and sparked international media attention. But it didn't mean much to the already shattered hookers strutting the shabby Prince George alleys. Social workers say the city is a magnet for children living in abusive, poor families on surrounding reserves and has long been known for its thriving prostitution business.

"The girls Ramsay preyed upon were all addicted to drugs and willing to risk everything to feed their habit and Ramsay knew it," Associate Chief Patrick Dohm said when handing down his sentence.

One of his victims, a 14-year-old known only as "A" whom he paid for oral sex, appeared in Ramsay's court eight times. Ramsay told her he would let her off easy if she kept quiet about what he liked to do with her and other teen prostitutes in the woods.

RCMP Cpl. Judy Thomas started hearing rumours about a deviant judge as early as 1999. The girls wouldn't even meet with her at first, said Thomas. It wasn't until the judge ruled against one of his victims in a child custody hearing that the woman went to police.

Beyond Ramsay's activities, social workers say the level of sexual exploitation in the community is dizzying. "We've always had very young women on the streets, very addicted women," said Linda Keefe, a local outreach worker. "I've been here 13 years and that has never changed." (Amy Carmichael, CP)

◄ Accompanied by his wife, David Ramsay arrives at court for sentencing on June 1, 2004. (Dave Milne/*Prince George Citizen*)

Nine Hells Angels and associates convicted of total of 26 criminal charges

In what one lawyer called a legal precedent in Canada, a jury in Montreal convicted nine Hells Angels and associates on gangsterism charges in March 2004, finding them guilty on 26 of 27 criminal charges.

The charges resulted from a police operation called Operation Springtime 2001, which ended seven years of battles in the streets of Montreal between the gangs fighting for control of the drug trade. About 150 people were killed in the turf war, including an 11-year-old boy who was struck by shrapnel from a car bomb as he played nearby.

The accused each faced charges of gangsterism, drug trafficking and conspiracy to commit murder. Eight of the men were convicted on all three counts, while the ninth was acquitted of the murder charge. They received prison terms ranging from 10 to 22 years.

"It's the first time anywhere in Canada a jury had to decide about a verdict on gangsterism," Crown prosecutor Madeleine Giauque said. The jurors had sorted through about 125 days of testimony in the year-long trial. Previous convictions on gangsterism were handed down by judges alone.

The trial, held at a specially built $16.5-million courthouse in Montreal's north end, was repeatedly described as one of the longest ever held in Canada. Giauque predicted there would be more such mega-trials. "Unfortunately, crime is organized in Quebec and I think that police, Justice Department officials, including the courts, have to be organized to deliver an efficient fight against organized crime."

The sentences were not the only ones to result from the major police crackdown on Quebec's biker gangs. A few days later, the Hells Angels were dealt another blow as two members of the notorious Nomads chapter received stiff sentences for importing drugs and plotting the killings of rival bikers. "The court should send a clear message to the accused that their conduct is unanimously condemned by the whole of society," said Quebec Superior Court Justice Gilles Hebert.

Justice officials who attempted to put Hells Angels members behind bars in Manitoba were not as successful in 2004. Charges against five Hells Angels associates, including conspiracy to commit murder and participating in a criminal organization, were stayed after the Crown's star witness decided not to testify against his former friends. Four of the bikers walked out of the Winnipeg Remand Centre to waiting stretch limos and a hero's welcome from family, friends and other bikers wearing their full colours.

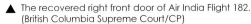

▲ The recovered right front door of Air India Flight 182.
(British Columbia Supreme Court/CP)

◀ The remains of two burned seats. (Chuck Stoody/CP)

Air India bombing trial slow to shed light

The long-running trial of two men charged in connection with the bombings on two Air India flights in 1985 that killed 331 people continued into its second year in 2004.

Ajaib Singh Bagri and Ripudaman Singh Malik faced conspiracy and murder charges in the bombings. The Crown alleged the two were part of a group of B.C. Sikh separatists who targeted India's national airline to retaliate against the Indian Army's attack a year earlier on the Golden Temple, Sikhism's holiest shrine.

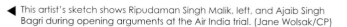

Air India flight 182 exploded off the coast of Ireland, killing 329 people, while two baggage handlers were killed when another bomb went off in a Tokyo airport. It was the most horrific terrorist act in Canadian history.

In November 2003, the star witness against Malik testified that the accused had confessed his involvement in the mass murder on at least two occasions. The woman, a former day-care supervisor at a school Malik headed, said her boss confided his darkest secret in her because the two had fallen in love. The defence depicted her as a jealous, jilted lover.

A month later, the Crown showed a videotaped speech by Bagri who called for young Sikhs to rise up and take revenge against the Indian government. Bagri, a fiery 34-year-old preacher in July 1984, rallied a crowd of frenzied Sikhs in New York, shouting: "Until we kill 50,000 Hindus we will not rest." Prosecutors said the speech showed motive for his involvement in the Air India bombings. The defence called its own translator to say Bagri's speech was just over-the-top rhetoric.

In February 2004, a female friend of Bagri's was dismissed from testifying after she said she couldn't recall the most basic details of her relationship with him. Crown prosecutor Richard Cairns pressed her for weeks to tell the court the same damning story she gave police about Bagri in a series of interviews that spanned more than a decade. Authorities said she had told them that Bagri came to her house on the eve of the terrorist attack to borrow her car to leave luggage at the airport. Suspicious of his plans, she refused. Then, she said he visited her a few days after the explosion and told her she knew his secret and could get him in big trouble.

The Crown wrapped up the main points of its case in May and the defence testimony began in June.

For the family members of those killed in the bombings, the long-running trial finally provided some answers amidst a lot of pain. At one point, families were invited to tour a warehouse where experts had attempted to reconstruct the plane with pieces scooped up from the sea. Mini Mamak, whose mother was killed, turned down the offer to see the charred seats and blackened windows her mother must have looked out of in the panic moments before she died. "I saw some of the pictures they sent us and just seeing those was so emotionally overwhelming," said Mamak. (Wendy Cox, Amy Carmichael, CP)

Crime and Punishment | 101

▲ Geoff Gaul, spokesman for the B.C. Crown prosecutors office, outside Kelly Ellard's trial. The office decided to go ahead with a third trial for Ellard. (Chuck Stoody/CP)

Notorious teen murder trial ends in mistrial; Kelly Ellard denies she killed fellow teen

Hopelessly deadlocked. The likelihood of a third trial. That's how one of Canada's most notorious murder trials ended, a case notable for its exposure of the savagery of some teen violence, particularly among girls.

Kelly Ellard's second trial for second-degree murder in the savage beating and drowning death of fellow teen Reena Virk in Victoria in 1997 came no closer to bringing the matter to rest than an earlier trial.

Ellard was sent to trial a second time after the B.C. Court of Appeal overturned a guilty verdict in the first trial in 2000 and ordered a new hearing, saying she

had not received a fair trial because Crown counsel had improperly cross-examined her. She pleaded not guilty at both trials.

What startled many when the beating and drowning of Virk first came to light was that all but one of the people involved were female teenagers. Ellard was 15. Six girls, who cannot be identified under youth protection laws, were convicted in 1998 of assault. The sole male charged, Warren Glowatski, was convicted in 1999 of second-degree murder and sentenced to life imprisonment with no parole consideration for seven years.

The horrifying story began on a chilly night on November 14, 1997, with a full moon and a clear sky near an ocean inlet known as the Gorge waterway. More than two dozen teens, including Virk, Ellard and Glowatski, gathered near the Gorge. An unsuspecting Virk, who was a troubled teen living in a foster home at the time, was invited by some of the girls who had a grudge against her to join them that night. Some of them confronted her and one girl stubbed a lit cigarette out on her forehead. Virk tried to leave, but she was surrounded and pummelled by a swarm of girls and Glowatski. She managed to stumble away from her attackers, making it across the Craigflower Bridge that spans the Gorge. Once there she was attacked again and drowned.

In her testimony, Ellard alternately sobbed and showed flashes of frustration, telling the Crown to stop asking the same questions. After she was shown a saltwater-stained jacket the Crown said she wore the night Virk died, she said, "I'm obviously going to be convicted."

But she was wrong. The jury of six men and six women announced after three days of deliberation that they were deadlocked. The judge asked them to try again, but a day later they sent word that they had "exhausted all avenues of deliberation." The jury said in a note: "We have reached an impasse that cannot result in a unanimous decision in spite of ANY further discussion."

The last chapter in this tragedy was still to be written; a third trial was pending. (Greg Joyce, CP)

▲ A police photo of marijuana plants growing inside an old brewery in Barrie, Ont. (Tobin Grimshaw/CP)

The sweet scent of money smells a lot like pot to grow-op owners

Mike Arsenault knew there was something strange about the posh house with the extra roof vents and permanently closed blinds. He said he could sometimes smell the sweet, pungent aroma of marijuana around the Moncton, N.B., home, but he never thought to call police.

His suspicions were confirmed when 13 people were arrested in raids on 14 homes in the Moncton area as part of an investigation into marijuana grow operations. RCMP seized 5,100 plants and more than 31 kg of dried pot.

From the courts to the cops, marijuana was big news in Canada in 2004. For police, marijuana production continued to be a persistent headache, with seizures averaging 1.1 million plants annually. For some police forces, investigations into marijuana grow operations represent more than half their drug cases, said an RCMP report. In Surrey, B.C., there were 658 grow-ops reported to police in 2002. In Winnipeg, 108 grow-ops were busted in 2003. In Ontario, police estimated 10,000 children were being raised in grow houses by "gardeners" or "crop sitters." The businesses are a big risk for fire, power outages, poisonous gases and explosions.

Perhaps the most dramatic discovery was the huge grow house—described as the largest in Canadian history—found by police in a former Molson's brewery in Barrie, Ont. Much of the illicit weed was being grown inside huge vats once used for beer production. Completely revamped and equipped with irrigation systems, timed lighting and ventilation hoses, the 40 or so vats served as self-contained environments. Police said pot was sprouting in some rooms as well and there was a complete dormitory outfitted to accommodate 50 people. Nine men were charged for the production and possession of marijuana.

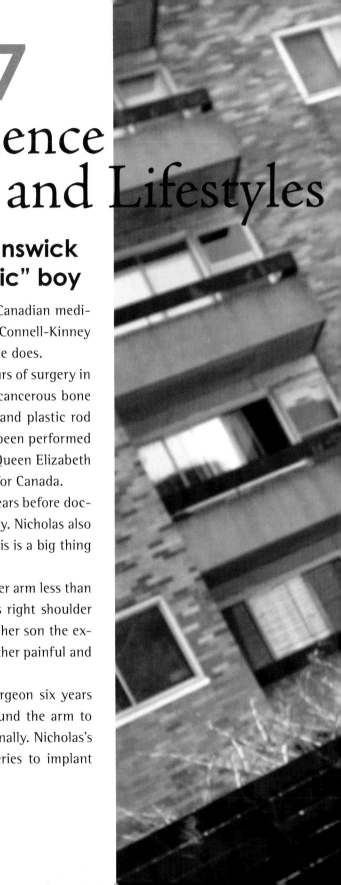

PART 7
Health, Science and Lifestyles

Grade 3 student from New Brunswick becomes Canada's first "bionic" boy

He was only nine years old, but he recorded a first for Canadian medical science. In May 2004, cancer patient Nicholas McConnell-Kinney received a "bionic" arm—a prosthesis that will grow as he does.

The child from Woodstock, N.B., underwent four hours of surgery in a ground-breaking operation that replaced 15.5 cm of cancerous bone in his upper arm bone with a spring-loaded, titanium and plastic rod that will grow as he grows. Although the operation has been performed about 20 times in the United States, the surgery at the Queen Elizabeth II Health Sciences Centre in Halifax was a medical first for Canada.

Orthopedic surgeon Michael Gross said it might be years before doctors could truly assess the ultimate success of the surgery. Nicholas also needed months of chemotherapy and rehabilitation. "This is a big thing for a small person," said Gross.

Doctors found a cancerous tumour in Nicholas's upper arm less than a month after he complained of a constant ache in his right shoulder bone. His mother, Cheri, praised the surgeon for giving her son the experimental treatment, which promises a life without further painful and intrusive limb-replacement surgeries.

The Repiphysis implant, developed by a French surgeon six years ago, expands when an electromagnetic coil is put around the arm to soften the plastic and slowly lengthen the implant internally. Nicholas's only other options were amputation or multiple surgeries to implant longer prostheses until adulthood. (*Halifax Daily News*)

In 2004 Nicholas McConnell-Kinney became the first Canadian recipient of a prosthesis that will grow as he does. (Christian Laforce/*Halifax Chronicle-Herald*)

Low-carb craze leads to new products on store shelves

North Americans trying to lose weight went crazy over low-carb diets in 2004. Diets such as the Atkins and the South Beach touted the effects of low or no carbohydrates—those starches and sugars found in a large number of foods. Such diets have been around for decades, but the newest craze had them challenging and changing the entire food industry. Companies making "high-carb" products such as pasta and other starchy and sugary foods found themselves out of favour, on store shelves and on the stock market. Potato farmers in Manitoba lost their contracts with a frozen potato processor and many said they would be forced out of farming.

It didn't take long for low-carb versions of everything from beer to bread to be invented. Both Pepsi and Coca-Cola announced the launch of drinks with half the carbohydrates of their regular versions of Coke and Pepsi. There was low-carb yogurt and low-carb tortillas, low-carb potatoes and low-carb chocolate bars.

Meanwhile, some companies that produced a lot of protein products saw a jump in sales. Maple Leaf Foods said its sales of meat from chicken and pigs saw some gains. Even in British Columbia, which endured a serious avian flu outbreak, low-carb dieters stayed loyal to barbecued chicken.

◀ Dietitian, and author, Vesanto Melina pours homemade low-carb salad dressing onto a salad in Langley, B.C., in 2004. (Richard Lam/CP)

Many nutritionists scoffed at the diet, saying its high fat content made it dangerous for people with heart conditions. And some researchers warned that it could trigger a sharp resurgence in devastating birth defects and childhood cancers. Bread, pasta, breakfast cereals and orange juice—largely shunned in low-carb diets—are key sources of folic acid, a micronutrient essential to the neurological development of fetuses.

Trans fat = bad fat = bad publicity

The dirty phrase in the food industry in 2004 was trans fat, and manufacturers scrambled to reduce or eliminate this type of fat from their products in advance of new government labelling regulations, effective in late 2005, that make the listing of calories and 13 key nutrients—including trans fat—mandatory.

"Some companies started avoiding trans fat when they learned the science many years ago," said Dr. Bruce Holub, a nutritional scientist at the University of Guelph. "Other companies waited until they had to confess them."

Although the public remained largely unaware of the issue for decades, developments in recent years—including a landmark study from Harvard University—have brought trans fat to the fore. Trans fat is made when manufacturers add hydrogen to vegetable oil—a process called hydrogenation. Holub tabled his first report to the government on trans fat in 1980.

"Every one gram of trans increased the risk of heart disease by approximately 20 per cent," said Holub of the results published in the Harvard study. "When you consider the average Canadian is consuming eight to 10 grams a day, you can see why we need to be really concerned about our extremely high trans intake in this country."

Among the companies that removed trans fat or declared their intention to do so in 2004 were Pepperidge Farms, the maker of Goldfish crackers; Frito-Lay; High Liner Foods; french-fry maker Cavendish Farms; Dare Foods; Voortman Cookies; and Kraft Foods, maker of Oreo cookies.

> "Every one gram of trans increased the risk of heart disease by approximately 20 per cent."

In May, McDonald's admitted to a Commons health committee that it hadn't yet met targets for reducing trans fat levels in its cooking oils. New York Fries offers trans-free fries at all its Canadian locations. (Greg Bonnell, CP)

Brian Feeney, right, pilot of the DaVinci Project, with X-Prize executive director Gregg Maryniak in 2004. (Aaron Harris/CP) ▶

Middle: Wild Fire rocket. (Aaron Harris/CP)
▼ Bottom: DaVinci Project pilot Brian Feeney. (Aaron Harris/CP)

Two Canadian teams enter contest to launch private spacecraft

The challenge: to safely launch and return a privately developed three-person craft 100 km into sub-orbital space twice within 14 days. The prize: $10 million. The competition: more than two dozen rockets from around the world, including a $20-million-plus project funded by Microsoft billionaire Paul G. Allen.

Those odds didn't deter two teams of Canadians from entering the Ansari X Prize competition, designed to encourage the development of private space travel. There was the Toronto-based da Vinci Project, which entered a bowling pin-shaped rocket, dubbed *Wild Fire.* Leader Brian Feeney described it as "a project with guts and excitement, that the average person can relate to." *Wild Fire*'s design was unique in that it fired its rockets from an altitude of 24,000 metres after being shuttled skyward by a reusable helium balloon. "We've considered every possible scenario of things going wrong," Feeney said. "Space has absolutely no sense of humour. I feel more than safe going up in it. It is a very, very solid craft."

Canada's second entry was from Canadian Arrow, a company based in London, Ont., and run by entrepreneur Geoff Sheerin, who has dreamed of transporting passengers into space since he was 14 years old. "You should try telling your high school guidance counsellor that you want to build spacecraft and launch people. It doesn't go over very well."

Canadian Arrow planned test flights of its spacecraft from a site near Lake Huron, while the da Vinci Project picked Kindersley, Sask., as its launch site. Neither were deterred in June 2004 when the California group got its SpaceShipOne project 100 km above Earth and safely home again, although it was not an official competition flight. "They have to take a look at the results of this flight and make sure they've got the technology matching what it takes to do the X Prize flight," said Sheerin. "Anyone could get this prize."

Online lotteries in Canada spark controversy

Atlantic Canadians were the first in Canada to be able to buy lottery tickets online in 2004, when the Atlantic Lottery Corp. started offering its tickets over the Internet.

Virtual ticket sales have been successful in more than 30 lottery associations worldwide, including most European countries, Australia and the United Kingdom.

Canadian legal restrictions required the corporation's site to have extensive checks and balances. Players needed to first register online, providing proof they were at least 19 years old, or 18 in P.E.I., and a resident of Atlantic Canada. A credit information company verifies the information.

Players transfer funds from online bank accounts into their website accounts to buy tickets for seven different lottery games. Credit card payments are not allowed. Winning ticket holders are sent an e-mail, and payouts of up to $1,000 are deposited into a player's existing account.

There is a weekly spending limit of between $1 and $99, set by players, and a function allowing players to block themselves from the website for anywhere from one day to one year.

Dr. Rina Gupta, co-director of McGill University's International Centre for Youth Gambling Problems, said the safety precautions don't go nearly far enough to combat problem gambling. "My concern is the blurring of what is gambling and where this could lead," she said. "It's absolutely gambling."

Bernie Walsh of Halifax lost his marriage, his home and his savings to a video lottery terminal addiction, and predicted the new service would "cost people dearly and not just money." He said, "Gambling has taken me down a long, dark road, and it's a scary road to come back from." (Susan Aitken, CP)

Same-sex marriages—and divorces—cause controversy

Wedding bells for gay newlyweds rang across Canada in 2004, as many couples didn't wait for the federal government to legalize gay marriage before saying, "I do". They were wed in several provinces that started issuing licences even before Canada's top court gave its opinion on Ottawa's draft legislation legalizing same-sex marriage across Canada.

Driven by lower court rulings saying laws banning gay marriage were unconstitutional, Quebec, British Columbia, the Yukon and Nova Scotia followed Ontario's lead in issuing gay marriage licences, while Manitoba also said it would not oppose a court bid by three same-sex couples who wanted to get married. Meanwhile, courts in other provinces were also being asked by gay couples to recognize same-sex marriages. It was a juggernaut that could not be stopped by either the federal government's desire to wait for the Supreme Court's view, or the opposition of many Canadians, both individuals and organizations such as the Roman Catholic Church.

An advocacy group for gays, Canadians For Equal Marriage,

▲ Michael Hendricks, left, and Rene Leboeuf celebrate becoming the first gay couple in Quebec to marry. (Paul Chiasson/CP)

said public and political opinion had changed and people were more accepting of gay marriage. "The more Canadians get to know their lesbian and gay neighbours, the less it is an issue," said spokeswoman Cicely McWilliam. "It just whittles away at fear and perhaps ignorance."

And, inevitably, perhaps, even before same-sex marriage was legal across the country, the first same-sex divorce was granted in Ontario. An Ontario Superior Court judge struck down the section of the Divorce Act that said only spouses—defined as a man and woman—can divorce and granted a lesbian couple in Toronto what was described by a lawyer as the first gay divorce in the world.

Battle over genetic seed patent goes to Supreme Court

It was a patent battle between a 73-year-old Saskatchewan farmer and a U.S. biotech giant, and the Supreme Court of Canada sided with the giant. The court ruled 5-4 in 2004 that Monsanto held a valid patent on a gene it inserted into canola plants to make them resistant to Roundup herbicide, and that canola farmer Percy Schmeiser infringed the patent by knowingly planting the Roundup Ready seeds.

Schmeiser said he collected and replanted his own seeds, which were accidentally cross-pollinated and contaminated with Monsanto's canola. The case made Schmeiser the international flag-bearer for environmental and agricultural groups opposed to genetically modified foods.

Lower courts had rejected Schmeiser's claim the canola landed on his fields by accident. But they didn't deal with the deeper issue of whether Monsanto could control a plant's use because it had a patent on a gene. Terry Sakreski, Schmeiser's lawyer, said while the high court decision brought the legal battle to a close, it did not end the war over the use of genetically modified plants. "I think this is a matter that Parliament needs seriously to look at," said Sakreski.

The high court said even though a plant is a higher life form and therefore cannot be patented, a gene in a plant can be, and that gives the patent-holder some rights over the plant's use. The minority of the court, however, said Monsanto should not be allowed to do indirectly what Canadian law has not allowed it to—acquire ownership protection over whole plants because of a gene patent.

Schmeiser did win a small victory. He didn't have to pay his earnings from his 1997 crop year to Monsanto, because he never sprayed the crop with Roundup, and therefore didn't profit from the patented gene. Neither did he have to pay Monsanto's legal costs. "I brought it as far as I could, all the way to the Supreme Court," said Schmeiser, whose speaking engagements around the world helped to defray legal costs he estimated at almost $500,000. "I'll always be fighting for the rights of farmers to be able to use their seed from year to year. So, the battle ends for me today, but not the battle in my heart."

Bare bellies everywhere

It was a year when fashion trends left bellies bare everywhere. For women, it was the combination of low-rise pants and tight cropped tops. For guys, saggy-bottomed pants several sizes too big made it only too clear what brand of boxers the wearer preferred.

The body and underwear-baring fashions spread like wildfire. Clothing manufacturers came up with labels such as super low-rise, ultra low-rise and extra low-rise for bottoms. Some school boards in Canada issued directives to keep skimpy clothes out of school hallways. In Louisiana, a politician sponsored a bill making it illegal to wear underwear-exposing pants. "There comes a time in every society where we must draw a line of decency," Democrat Derrick Shepherd said in a fiery speech.

◀ Bare midriffs were everywhere in 2004, including on the runway at Fashion Week in Toronto in March. (Adrian Wyld/CP)

But there seemed to be good news on the horizon for those sick of belly buttons. Fall fashion trends suggested waistbands were creeping upward—not that they could have gone any lower—and tight tops were layered with dress shirts and sweaters, and covered up with—of all things—ponchos. How long that trend would last was open to question, however. "I have a funny feeling that we're just going to get sick to death of that poncho really soon, but right now it's everywhere and it looks great," said Robin Keeler, fashion director at Toronto's Yorkdale Shopping Centre.

Spam: E-mail nightmare lurks in desktops everywhere

E-mail seemed like such a convenience when it was first introduced. You could communicate with people around the world, within seconds, without major cost. It was a great way to reach out to people who would be otherwise unreachable.

Then came spam. The Internet's version of junk mail is estimated to be as much as 80 per cent of all e-mail, and clearing out spam from e-mail accounts became a huge time-waster for many Canadians in 2004.

"Canada is the second source of spam worldwide behind the United States and risks becoming a spam haven unless action is taken," said panel member Michael Geist, an e-commerce legal expert at the University of Ottawa. But Geist said existing legislation could put a dent in the spam if only it were applied.

Internet companies, meanwhile, scrambled to keep ahead of the spam artists with screening software and patches to existing programs. In the United States, large e-mail providers launched lawsuits to crack down on unsolicited e-mail.

The Internet's version of junk mail is estimated to be as much as 80 per cent of all e-mail.

The federal government created a panel of experts to come up with an anti-spam plan and said it would pass tougher laws if necessary to fight what it called the undermining of the Internet. It saps productivity and ties up Internet traffic. Internet providers, cable company representatives and scholars were asked to submit a game plan on the problem.

But the only solution that seemed to work reliably was the delete button. (Dan Dugas, CP)

Worries about West Nile disease fade as summer passes

With the number of public health scares sweeping the country, purveyors of black humour joked that a Canadian was someone who had sworn off beef, adopted hospital masks as their fashion accessory of choice and given up chi-chi colognes for a liberal dousing of eau de DEET.

Mad cow disease. SARS. West Nile disease. The huge health concerns of 2003 seem to fade in 2004. Or did they? In the case of West Nile, it was true that at the height of summer there still had been no human cases of the mosquito-borne disease and dead birds testing positive for the virus had been found in just four provinces. But experts said that when it comes to West Nile, which can cause a condition similar to meningitis, Canadians weren't out of the woods.

Still, the not-in-my-backyard attitude seemed to be prevalent, a Health Canada report suggested in mid-spring. It found that just four in 10 Canadians were taking steps to protect themselves from the disease. "I think the difficulty here is that folks may not necessarily appreciate how bad West Nile virus can be," said Dr. Karim Kurji, associate chief medical officer of health for Ontario. "While in the majority of incidents it may be relatively symptom-less, we know that in one in 150 individuals it can be very severe and lead to many debilitating effects."

In 2003, 1,200 Canadians were diagnosed with West Nile disease and 10 of them died, most in Saskatchewan. That year seven provinces—Nova Scotia, New Brunswick, Quebec, Ontario, Manitoba, Saskatchewan and Alberta—also reported West Nile activity, either in birds, mosquitoes or humans or a combination of the three. By mid-2004, the virus had been detected in fewer than 100 dead birds in Quebec, Ontario, Manitoba and Saskatchewan. Unseasonably cool temperatures across much of the country may have been one reason why West Nile stayed simmering at low levels. (Sheryl Ubelacker, CP)

Fears about flu end quickly, but long-term planning continues

▲ Scotia Nutt, 5, of Wallaceburg, Ont., gets her annual flu shot in December 2003. (Diana Martin/*Chatham Daily News*)

It started early and it started hard. But the upside of the year's nasty flu season was that it came to an early—and welcome—end. By January 2004, influenza figures from Health Canada showed the flu season had peaked in most parts of the country, except for Quebec and New Brunswick, where activity peaked a little later.

Flu season in Canada runs from November until April and usually hits between 10 and 25 per cent of Canadians. Although Canadians escaped relatively unscathed in 2004, the issue of whether the country was ready to deal with an influenza pandemic continued to be at the forefront of Health Canada's to-do list. In February 2004 it unveiled its pandemic flu plan, which had been in the works since 1988. The plan is designed to reduce deaths due to influenza and to try to minimize the social disruption that a period of mass illness would cause. It is estimated that anywhere between 4.5 million and 10.6 million Canadians could fall ill in a short period of time during a flu pandemic, with between 11,000 and 58,000 of them dying.

The plan anticipated a staggering array of potential problems, from overwhelmed hospitals, overcrowded morgues and difficulties maintaining essential services. The World Health Organization hailed the blueprint, saying "no other country has an equally far advanced plan." (Helen Branswell, CP)

▲ Don Appleby, a marijuana prescription holder, protests the government's restrictions on marijuana on Parliament Hill in 2003. (Jonathan Hayward/CP)

More Canadians turn to marijuana

The proportion of Canadians who admit to indulging in marijuana or hashish almost doubled over the past 13 years—and the highest rates of use were among teens. That translates into about three million Canadians, or 12.2 per cent, who used cannabis at least once in the previous year, Statistics Canada said in a community health survey released in 2004. In 1989, the figure was 6.5 per cent.

The hike in marijuana's popularity came as no surprise to Edward Adlaf, a research scientist at the Centre for Addiction and Mental Health in Toronto, which has reported similar trends, particularly from its surveys of Ontario students. "We've been finding during the '90s among students—and these are sev-

enth graders to 12th graders—that fewer and fewer students perceive great risk in using cannabis."

A sea-change in perceived risk—called "generational forgetting"—was believed to be behind a resurgence in cocaine and crack use among teenagers, said Adlaf, explaining that most adolescents today have no experience with adverse cocaine effects, unlike students in the 1980s, who saw the death of U.S. comedian John Belushi, for instance. Yet more recent deaths from ecstasy appear to have turned many teens against the so-called rave drug, said Adlaf.

The Statistics Canada study revealed that increased drug use hasn't been confined to cannabis, which includes marijuana, hashish and hash oil. The survey also found that a higher proportion of Canadians were taking other illegal drugs: cocaine or crack, ecstasy, LSD and other hallucinogens, amphetamines (speed) and heroin. Overall, 2.4 per cent of the survey's almost 37,000 respondents, all aged 15 or older, reported using at least one of these other drugs in the previous year, up from 1.6 per cent in 1994. And 1.3 per cent, or an estimated 321,000 Canadians, had used cocaine or crack, making it the most commonly used of these illicit, harder drugs.

A loosening-up in attitudes towards pot may have contributed to more people smoking up—or admitting that they do. Greater availability of the leaf may also come into play. (Sheryl Ubelacker, CP)

Survey of youth contradicts image of troubled, unruly teenagers

Most Canadian teens enjoy school, get along with their parents, have part-time jobs and don't often get depressed, according to a study conducted for Health Canada. The study, based on a 2003 survey, contradicted the popular image of surly adolescents locked in a universal war with the authority figures in their life.

study conducted by GPC Research of Ottawa. "Most teens do not want to disappoint their parents."

Most (82 per cent) said they felt part of the school they attend and participate in extracurricular activities (70 per cent). But boys were less likely than girls to enjoy school (66 versus 77 per cent). More than two-thirds of teens said their parent or guard-

More than two-thirds of teens said their parent or guardian takes a lot of interest in their school work.

The survey did confirm one commonly held belief about teens: that they are risk-takers. It said approximately a third of those surveyed had tried marijuana more than once, and one in 10 had tried magic mushrooms. Usage of other drugs was lower: Four per cent said they had tried ecstasy; three per cent had tried crack cocaine or glue-sniffing; 2 per cent, crystal meth; 1 per cent, heroin.

"Overall, Canadian teens perceive themselves having a good relationship with their parents," says the

ian takes a lot of interest in their school work.

There were worrisome findings, too. More than half, 55 per cent, said they had a hard time concentrating, 51 per cent said they get bored easily and 63 per cent worried a lot about their future.

And the survey confirmed that teens spend a lot of time with the mass media: 63 per cent watched two or more hours of television daily, while 10 per cent of respondents said they surfed the Internet for five or more hours daily. (Dennis Bueckert, CP)

PART 8
Canada Around the World

Canadian Forces safeguard security in Kabul

About 2,000 Canadians went to Kabul in August 2003 as part of NATO's International Security Assistance Force. Canada was the largest single contributor to the 34-country, 5,000-member contingent helping restore security in the Afghan capital.

Initially charged with patrolling the Afghan capital's southwest sector, the Canadians' area of operations more than doubled in size the night before they assumed responsibility from a smaller German battalion. The Canadian sector included not only crowded city streets and village-type markets, but goat tracks and mountain passes, dusty desert and fertile valleys extending far beyond their base, Camp Julien, on the city's southern fringe.

On October 2, three Canadians driving along a goat track in an unarmoured Iltis jeep struck newly planted anti-tank mines. Two soldiers were killed. Another soldier riding with them was wounded along with two more in a second Iltis.

Maj.-Gen. Andrew Leslie, the contingent commander and the security force's deputy chief, soon shored up the Canadians' fleet of armoured vehicles and redistributed the three companies of the 3rd Battalion, Royal Canadian Regiment Battle Group. Armoured troops moved into rural areas previously patrolled by the battalion's Para Company, while the paratroopers and a company of regular light infantry were restricted to the hard ground of the city proper. Ottawa also accelerated the purchase of armoured Mercedes G-Wagons. Though they would not withstand anti-tank mines, the sturdier new vehicles still gave the troops an added measure of security against less powerful weapons.

By January, the Canadians had begun participating in so-called directed operations, or raids, backing up city police and national security officers as

A group of Afghan children share a laugh with Cpl. Greg Soucy of Quebec City in the streets of Kabul in July. (Stephen Thorne/CP) ▶

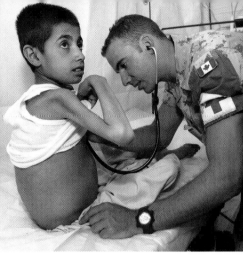

Canadian Forces Cpl. Kevin Comeau examines Djamshid at the military hospital in Kabul, Afghanistan, in June. (Stephen Thorne/CP)

Djamshid Djan Popal, second from right, and his father Shafiullah, second from left, say goodbye to relatives before they leave Afghanistan to seek medical treatment in Canada for Djamshid. (Stephen Thorne/CP)

they entered suspected criminal and terrorist compounds. Two raids late in the month are believed to have sparked a suicide bomb attack January 27 that killed a Canadian soldier and wounded three others—all riding in an open Iltis just days before they were to go home.

With Canadian Lt.-Gen. Rick Hillier now at ISAF's helm and the arrival of the 3rd Battalion, Royal 22nd Regiment Battle Group, along with armoured reconnaisance troops, the Canadians began shifting their attention outward. Most patrols were conducted in armoured vehicles or the new G-Wagons, whose roomy, air-conditioned interiors more than compensated for the fact their roofs didn't retract and bulletproof windows didn't open.

Working on behalf of the Kabul Multi-National Brigade, a Canadian-commanded pool of ISAF resources, reconnaissance troops regularly ventured in their Coyote armoured vehicles north and south into Taliban country. They collected intelligence, hobnobbed with village elders and established temporary medical clinics, the first of which unearthed the case of Djamshid

Djan Popal, a nine-year-old Afghan boy with rheumatic heart disease. With a sponsor in Hamilton willing to pay his way, Canadian military doctors arranged medical care for the boy in Ontario.

The Canadians found no Taliban on the reconnaissance missions, but infantry assisted in the capture of some suspected terrorists during several raids closer to their main camp.

By spring, Ottawa had committed to another year in Afghanistan, though with a smaller force of 700. The original 2,000-member Canadian contingent left Kabul in August 2004. Norwegians, Belgians and Hungarians took over the Canadian sector, leasing space at Camp Julien, and Hillier handed command of the security force to a French general.

Ottawa's commitment to Afghanistan was not limited to military. On the humanitarian side, it pledged more than $300 million to Afghan reconstruction over three years, making Afghanistan the largest single beneficiary of Canadian aid. (Stephen Thorne, CP)

New prime minister abroad

The first foreign trip Paul Martin embarked on as prime minister was to a January summit of the 34-member Organization of American States, in Mexico, where Canada joined Latin American countries and the United States in discussing regional issues ranging from free trade to anti-corruption measures.

U.S. President George W. Bush was at the summit in Monterrey, Mexico, but it was in April, when Martin made an official visit to Washington, that the two had more time to sit down and talk in depth about Canada-U.S. relations. "We certainly got along very well," Martin said after meeting Bush at the White House. High on the agenda for their discussion was Canada's desire for a speedy end to the U.S. ban on live Canadian cattle imports, imposed after the discovery of a case of mad cow disease in Alberta in May 2003.

But the ban was still in place two months later when Martin and Bush were both participants at another summit—leaders of the Group of Eight industrialized countries meeting on Sea Island, off Savannah, Georgia. The G-8 summit was focused on wider issues such as the conflict in Iraq. It came during the federal election campaign in Canada and Martin left a day early to resume campaigning. (Paul Loong, CP)

Prime Minister Paul Martin and U.S. President George Bush take part in the official photo at the Summit of the Americas in Monterrey, Mexico in January. (Tom Hanson/CP)

Canadian Forces general revisits Rwanda horror at UN tribunal

In 1994 Lt.-Gen. Romeo Dallaire was head of a small UN peacekeeping force that had neither the mandate nor the manpower to stop one of the most horrific bloodbaths in Africa—the Rwandan genocide.

The country's Hutu majority tried to wipe out the minority Tutsi population. Hundreds of thousands were murdered, many brutally hacked to death. Most victims were Tutsis, but large numbers of politically moderate Hutus and others were among those who perished in massacres that went on unchecked for some 100 days.

Dallaire was hailed as a hero in some quarters for having tried to forestall the massacres, but his warnings went unheeded by superiors at the United Nations, and major world powers took little interest as the disaster loomed. The UN force he led was powerless when the genocide unfolded. The experience left him with deep psychological scars. He suffered from post-traumatic stress and had flashbacks to the horrors he witnessed. Once he was able to function normally again, Dallaire described his days in Rwanda as a descent into hell.

It was a journey that he was to relive at least twice—first when nightmarish memories flooded back as he was writing his book, *Shake Hands With the Devil: the Failure of Humanity in Rwanda*; and again when he testified against the alleged mastermind of the genocide.

Dallaire took the stand in January 2004 in Arusha, Tanzania, as a key witness at the UN tribunal prosecuting former Rwandan officials on charges of genocide and crimes against humanity. Among the accused was Col. Theoneste Bagosora, who allegedly orchestrated the massacres after seizing control of the Rwandan army and government in April 1994. Several months after his testimony, Dallaire told an interviewer that his face-to-face encounter with Bagosora at the tribunal was gut wrenching—his third descent into hell. (Paul Loong, CP)

Death of Canadian photojournalist strains Canada-Iran ties

The death of Montreal-based photojournalist Zahra Kazemi in 2003 in Iran opened up a major rift in relations between Canada and Iran. Kazemi, a Canadian citizen born in Iran, had been taken into custody for photographing a demonstration outside a prison. Her body was buried in Iran although her son wanted the body returned to Canada.

Iranian authorities at first said she died of a stroke. Under pressure to investigate, a committee formed by reformist President Mohammad Khatami later concluded that she died from a blow to the head and a prison official was charged. But the judiciary—controlled by hardliners—quickly cleared the official of wrongdoing and a counter-espionage intelligence official was charged with "semi-premeditated murder." He pleaded not guilty.

When Tehran refused to let Canadian diplomats attend the trial in July 2004, Ottawa threatened to recall its ambassador. In a surprise move, Canadian Ambassador Philip MacKinnon was allowed into the courtroom on the first day. The next day, the Canadian ambassador and other foreign observers were barred from the court and the trial was brought to an end abruptly. MacKinnon was recalled immediately to Ottawa to protest "this flagrant denial of due process."

A week later, the court acquitted the accused but offered monetary compensation to Kazemi's family, which they rejected. The judiciary claimed later that Kazemi's death was the result of an accidental fall, but Canada discounted the claim. "We want the truth," said Foreign Affairs Minister Pierre Pettigrew. (Paul Loong, CP)

◀ Philip MacKinnon, right, Canada's ambassador to Tehran, and the Dutch ambassador jump a rope outside an Iranian courthouse after they are blocked from attending the trial of a man charged in the death of a Canadian journalist. (Hasan Sarbakhshian/AP)

▲ Prime Minister Paul Martin, left, and President George W. Bush meet the media in Washington in April. (Jonathan Hayward/CP)

Canada stays out of Iraq invasion

With the benefit of hindsight, Jean Chrétien said he had no regrets over one of the toughest decisions he had to make while he was prime minister: Canada opted against sending troops to support the U.S.-led invasion of Iraq in March 2003.

The decision drew the ire of the U.S. administration, which wanted as many allies as possible to join the campaign against Saddam Hussein, the Iraqi president whose brutal regime was suspected of developing biological, chemical and even nuclear weapons.

But a year later—with no weapons of mass destruction found and deadly attacks against U.S.-led coalition forces raging almost daily in Iraq—Chrétien was glad he kept Canadian soldiers out of the quagmire. "The Canadian people are very pleased with the decision and feel very good about it, and it was a good occasion, too, to prove our independence," Chrétien said in March 2004.

Still, a number of individual Canadians were caught up in the turmoil.

Two Canadians were killed and five injured when a truck-bomb blew up at UN headquarters in Baghdad in August 2003. A month later, a Canadian television soundman was slightly injured in a bomb blast at a hotel. Another Canadian who worked as a security guard for foreign engineers at a power station in Mosul was killed by gunmen in March 2004. As well, several Canadians were kidnapped in Iraq during the year; at least two of them were subsequently released by their captors.

Even though Canadian troops stayed away from Iraq, Canada contributed $300 million for training Iraqi police officers and establishing other civil services such as law courts. Canada also forgave about $750 million in Iraqi debts to ease the country's financial burden.

Former prime minister delivers eulogy at former U.S. president's funeral

"Ronald Reagan does not enter history tentatively; he does so with certainty and panache," Brian Mulroney said at the June 11 funeral of the 40th U.S. president. "At home and on the world stage, his were not the pallid etchings of a timorous politician. They were the bold strokes of a confident and accomplished leader."

Reagan died at age 93, succumbing to pneumonia after suffering from Alzheimer's disease in his final years. Reagan's era in the White House spanned the 1980s, and Mulroney was prime minister in Canada during much of that period. The two enjoyed a warm friendship that was illustrated in public when they joined in a chorus of *When Irish Eyes Are Smiling* at a gala closing a Quebec City summit in 1985.

◀ Brian Mulroney and his wife Mila pause at the coffin of Ronald Reagan in the Capitol rotunda in Washington in June. (Ron Edmonds/AP)

Canadian veterans remember D-Day

Canada's Second World War veterans—some stooped by age, others pushed in wheelchairs or walking with the help of canes—returned to Normandy's beaches on June 6, 2004, to mark the 60th anniversary of D-Day. For some, it would be the final trek to the beaches of France that played a turning point in the Second World War,

At a ceremony on Juno Beach in the town of Courseulles-Sur-Mer, Canada's D-Day veterans were honoured by Queen Elizabeth II and Prime Minister Paul Martin for their sacrifice in fighting their way ashore amid a hail of Nazi gunfire during the Allied

◀ A Canadian veteran walks Juno Beach on the 60th anniversary of the D-Day landings. (Mike Large/NPA/Pool)

landings on that day in 1944.

Canada's military played a key role in the landings, code-named Operation Overlord, with about 18,000 troops storming ashore at Juno Beach. They suffered 1,074 casualties that day.

In total, the Allies lost 2,500 troops on D-Day, but the mission was a success as they gained the vital foothold they needed to drive the Nazis from France. The Battle of Normandy was to last almost three months, a campaign that left 20,000 Canadians dead or wounded.

For the survivors, the return to France brought back difficult memories.

"We made it through, some of us," said Ted O'Halloran, who was among the first wave of soldiers

▲ Dressed in an authentic British uniform, a soldier visits the Canadian military cemetery near Reviers, France. (Adrian Wyld/CP)

to hit the 8 km stretch of beach—between the towns of Saint-Aubin-Sur-Mer and Courseulles-Sur-Mer—that was code-named Juno by the Allies.

At the end of the ceremony, the veterans were given the chance to wander the beach alone. "It was really sad, but it was nice to be back, to see it again." said O'Halloran, who was 21 years old on D-Day.

During Canada's commemoration service attended by about 6,000 veterans, their families and local residents, the Queen reflected on the distance young Canadian soldiers had come to help end the Nazi occupation of Europe. "Britain had been directly threatened by the enemy, but you came across the Atlantic from the relative security of your homeland to fight for the freedom of Europe," she said.

For Doug Vidler, 80, it was the memory of those who never returned home that struck him hardest. "When I think about the guys we lost, I can't think about individuals; I go to pieces," said Vidler, who served in the Stormont, Dundas and Glengary Highlanders. (Kevin Ward, CP)

U.S. air force reprimands pilot who bombed Canadians

The U.S. air force did not mince words for one of its own "Top Gun" flyers who dropped a 225 kg laser-guided bomb on Canadian troops in Afghanistan in April 2002.

Maj. Harry Schmidt, a decorated F-16 fighter pilot, "acted shamefully ... exhibiting arrogance and a lack of flight discipline" in the bombing that killed four Canadians and wounded eight others, said Lt.-Gen. Bruce Carlson, who reprimanded Schmidt for dereliction of duty in July 2004.

Schmidt was fined US$5,672, equivalent to one month's salary. He also agreed he would never fly air force jets again.

Schmidt maintained throughout the proceedings that the so-called friendly-fire event was an accident. He insisted his superiors never told him Canadians were conducting a live-fire exercise at the Tarnak Farms firing range outside Kandahar on that fateful night, and he thought Afghanistan's Taliban militants were firing on his aircraft.

Carlson's reprimand said Schmidt used "the inherent right of self-defence as an excuse to wage your own war." Instead of attacking, Schmidt should have taken evasive action and flown his plane out of the range of the perceived danger, Carlson said.

Cpl. Roscoe Wiseman, from Teslin, Yukon, patrols in Port-au-Prince, Haiti in March. (Ryan Remiorz /CP)

Canadian troops keep peace in post-Aristide Haiti

A wave of violence swept across Haiti in early 2004 after the killing of a gang leader whose supporters blamed his death on the government of Jean-Bertrand Aristide. By February, gunmen were roaming across the Caribbean country, killing police officers and burning government buildings.

Aristide was powerless to stop the rebellion. Support for him had dwindled after he used a flawed election in 2000 to stay in power. Opponents accused his government of involvement in a wide range of misdeeds including gang violence, drug trafficking and corruption. Aristide fled on February 29, and left behind a power vacuum that opened the way for widespread looting, revenge killings and lawlessness.

Canada, Chile, France and the United States sent troops in a multinational effort to restore order.

A handful of elite special forces troops were the first Canadians to arrive. They were soon joined by members of the 2nd Royal Canadian Regiment from CFB Gagetown, N.B., six Griffin helicopters of the 430th Tactical Squadron based at CFB Valcartier, Que., along with military engineers and command and support elements—a total of some 500 military personnel.

Canadians began patrolling Port-au-Prince, Haiti's capital, in March. By April, they reported the situation had become more stable. "We've witnessed the return of Haitians back to their normal daily lifestyles and routine, unabated by previous criminal threats that existed prior to our arrival," said Lt.-Col. Jim Davis, commander of the Canadian contingent.

The mission, originally 90 days, was extended by two months—until August—to give the United Nations time to deploy up to 8,000 peacekeepers to replace the troops already in Haiti.

In July, Canada announced it would send 100 police officers to help improve security. Ottawa also committed more than $180 million over two years to reconstruction and development projects in Haiti. "We have a very large Haitian population in Canada and we do feel a hemispheric and moral responsibility," said Prime Minister Paul Martin. (Paul Loong, CP)

▲ Pvt. Matt Elliott, from Halifax, on patrol in the Carrefour district of Port-au-Prince in March. (Ryan Remiorz/CP)

JUNO CANADA'S MUSIC AWARDS

Sam Roberts, front, with his band members after winning three awards at the Junos in April. (Adrian Wyld/CP)

Arts & Entertainment

Nickelback and Sam Roberts win big at Junos

Juno fever hit a gusher in Canada's oil province when a record number of fans watched Sam Roberts, Sarah McLachlan and Nickelback pick up their hardware at the 2004 Juno music awards in Edmonton.

Alanis Morissette, host of the show, shocked viewers when she dropped a white robe to reveal a nude-coloured body suit with pasties covering her breasts. "I'm overjoyed to be back in my homeland, the true north, strong and censor-free," she said in an apparent reference to the aftermath caused by Janet Jackson's nipple exposure at the Super Bowl a few months earlier.

With three statuettes—all in major categories—Roberts was the biggest winner of the night. The Montrealer won every category he was nominated in, including the top prize of Artist of the Year. His debut record *We Were Born in a Flame*, which included the hit songs "Brother Down" and "Don't Walk Away Eileen," took Album of the Year and Rock Album of the Year.

"What an award represents to me more than anything is a life in music and for that I am very, very, very thankful," said Roberts. "The second album all of a sudden feels as heavy as the ring on poor Frodo's shoulders. I don't really know what we're going to do from here."

Nickelback, originally formed in Hanna, Alta., about 200 km northeast of Calgary, was welcomed home with statuettes for Group of the Year and Fan's Choice award. "These always feel so incredible, but it feels so much more to receive one of these at home," said frontman Chad Kroeger.

McLachlan had the happy task of making room in her suitcase for the Songwriter of the Year trophy, alongside the award for Best Pop Album. "I've been gone quite a long time . . . to come back and have this kind of love it feels really, really amazing," she said.

▲ Nelly Furtado performs on stage during the Juno Awards in Edmonton. (Jeff McIntosh/CP)

The show was stuffed full of live music, including Kathleen Edwards, Blackie & the Rodeo Kings, Avril Lavigne, the Barenaked Ladies and Aaron Lines. Nelly Furtado gave the best performance of the night with a melody of "Try" and "Powerless." She was accompanied by aboriginal group White Fish Juniors while more than 100 extras carrying placards reading "spirit" paraded through the audience. "You have the power to say something, you might as well do it in a cool way," Furtado said backstage. "It was really important to have an aboriginal drum group because it was part of the inspiration for the song 'Powerless.'" "Powerless" was named Single of the Year, while rock outfit Billy Talent from Toronto was crowned Best New Group.

An appearance by leather-clad Alice Cooper sent the audience into a frenzy. The shock rocker inducted Bob Ezrin, who produced Cooper's albums, into the Canadian Music Hall of Fame. "I met Bob over 30 years ago. We were just five guys from Detroit wearing our girlfriends' dresses looking for a record deal and a producer," said Cooper. (Angela Pacienza, CP)

Denys Arcand invades awards shows

Director Denys Arcand's *The Barbarian Invasions* became the most-honoured film in Canadian history in 2004, with a year of accolades topped off by an Academy Award as best foreign-language film.

Arcand's screenplay was a sequel to his earlier hit film, *Decline of the American Empire*, with most of the original actors returning. Critics and audiences alike adored the funny, pungent and poignant film focused on Remy, a cranky, terminally ill university professor who has an opportunity to reconcile with his estranged son. Meanwhile, a bunch of his old leftist cronies gather for what amounts to a wake. They revel in recollections of their hedonistic youth, when they experimented with all of the "isms" in Quebec, from socialism to feminism to separatism.

A few weeks after the Oscars, Arcand was again at the podium, accepting Genie awards, Canada's Oscar equivalent, including best picture, best director and screenplay. The film's stars, Remy Girard, Stephane Rousseau and Marie-Josée Croze, also took the best actor, best supporting actor and actress awards.

Arcand said the secret to success is all in the timing, namely to make a film "during the years that David (Cronenberg) and Atom (Egoyan) are inactive."

The Barbarian Invasions also took three César awards, France's film prizes—Best Film, Best Director and Best Original Screenplay.

Another Canadian saw success at the Academy Awards. Toronto native Howard Shore won for his musical score for *Lord of the Rings: Return of the King*. He also shared an Oscar with Fran Walsh and singer Annie Lennox for the winning song, "Into the West," from *Return of the King*.

Canadians also provided some of the musical entertainment on the televised show. In full character from the folk-music parody *A Mighty Wind*, Canucks Eugene Levy and Catherine O'Hara performed the Oscar-nominated song "A Kiss at the End of the Rainbow." Montreal jazz guitarist Benoît Charest and vocalist Sylvain Chomet also led an energetic and colourfully costumed ragtime version of Charest's nominated song from *The Triplets of Belleville*, "Belleville Rendez-vous," that had the audience tapping their feet in rhythm. (John McKay, CP)

Denys Arcand holds his Oscar for Best Foreign Film at the 76th annual Academy Awards. (Laura Rauch/AP)

Happy billionaire welcomes home his ivories

It was the Case of the Missing Ivories, and no one was happier when it was solved than Canada's richest man.

The palm-sized sculptures, the work of famed 18th-century portraitist David Le Marchand and owned by billionaire Ken Thomson, were on loan to the Art Gallery of Ontario in Toronto when they were stolen in mid-January 2004. They were anonymously returned— through a lawyer's office—about two weeks later.

A relieved and emotional Thomson, not known for speaking publicly about personal matters, told a news conference that he was "so, so happy" for the safe return of his art that he planned to sleep with the sculptures on their first night home.

It was not clear where the ivories had been or how they were kept during their two-week sojourn out of the display case. But save for a missing thumb on one of the portraits, the pieces were returned in their original condition.

Conan O'Brien befriends Canada

▼ Conan O'Brien gestures to fans on the street outside MuchMusic's studio in Toronto in February. (Frank Gunn/CP)

It was all fun and games when American TV host Conan O'Brien brought his late-night talk show to Canada—until he insulted French-Canadians.

O'Brien spent a week taping his NBC show *Late Night* at the downtown Elgin Theatre in Toronto, delighting his audience with monologues and sketches that riffed on Canadian themes, from beer to hockey to Mounties. O'Brien came to Toronto with the help of $1 million in taxpayers' money, some from the province of Ontario and some from a federal fund set up to help Toronto's tourist industry recover from SARS.

On the Thursday show, *Late Night* regular Triumph—a cigar-chomping, politically incorrect puppet—was dispatched to the Quebec winter carnival to take on Quebecers in general and separatists in particular. "So you're French and Canadian, yes? So you're obnoxious and dull," the puppet told one passerby. "You're in North America, learn the language," he hollered at another.

Some federal politicians expressed outrage about the sketch, and the president of Société Saint-Jean-Baptiste was not amused either. "It seems the governments of Canada, Ontario and Toronto sponsored it," Jean Dorion said of the show. "If that's the case, these administrations must dissociate themselves immediately from the program and apologize to Quebecers."

O'Brien, meanwhile, responded with more humour. On a later show, with a French translator by his side, he apologized. "People of Quebec, I'm sorry," O'Brien said in English. That was translated and subtitled to: "People of Quebec, I'm an albino jackass." O'Brien went on to say: "We meant no harm with our comedy piece the other night." That was translated into: "The other night, I wet the bed like a little girl." The comic then said: "I was a stranger in a strange land and I was very insensitive." Translated, his comments read: "I have a small penis."

Later, he invited famed French-Canadian entomologist Georges Brossard to the show. Brossard punished him for the earlier joke by bringing along a few of his multi-legged friends and placing them all over the clearly nervous O'Brien. At one point, O'Brien had everything from giant cockroaches to a tarantula crawling over his suit and head.

When it was all over, Brossard not only shook O'Brien's hand but hugged him. "Now we're friends," he said. (John McKay, CP)

Glitz, red carpet of Oscar night replicated at Canada's Walk of Fame ceremony

Jim Carrey poses with Mounties at Canada's ▼ Walk of Fame in Toronto. (Frank Gunn/CP)

They cried "Mario! Mario! Mario!" And they sang "Born to Be Wild!" But mostly and loudly they chanted "Jim, we love you!"

A thousand screaming fans waited for hours in bleachers outside Toronto's Roy Thomson Hall for the official arrivals onto the red carpet of the 2004 inductees into Canada's Walk of Fame.

Actor Jim Carrey's limousine was the last to arrive and he didn't disappoint, shaking hands and signing autographs for the delirious hometown fans. "I'm so glad to finally get a chance to say to the Canadian people how much they mean to me and how wonderful the whole trip has been," he told the crowd. "I couldn't have done it without you."

Carrey didn't just unveil his plaque. He yanked the cover off with the flourish of a matador and then sat atop it while his family flanked him for the photographers. "It's the whole DNA strain!" he shouted with a laugh.

NHL superstar Mario Lemieux had his own cheering section, many sporting Pittsburgh Penguins jerseys. "Obviously it's a great honour," Lemieux said. "I had

Actress Helen Shaver and hockey star Mario Lemieux pose with their stars. (Frank Gunn/CP)

a chance to be inducted into the Hockey Hall of Fame a few years ago but this is very special."

The arrival of Steppenwolf founder John Kay was greeted by an impromptu version of "Born to be Wild," a rock anthem made legend by the band. Dressed in black, Kay was accompanied by his official presenter, old friend Peter Fonda, whose motorcycle film *Easy Rider* featured the hit song. Also honoured with stars on the walk were actor and social activist Shirley Douglas, actor-director Helen Shaver, jazz performer Diana Krall and director Denys Arcand.

There were posthumous inductions for four pioneers of Hollywood who had Canadian roots: studio bosses Jack Warner and Louis B. Mayer, producer Mack Sennett and silent screen star Mary Pickford. Filmmaker Norman Jewison helped with the tribute to the so-called Canadian Connection. He said the 2004 event was a much bigger deal than the debut year in 1998 when he got his star. "There was 30 people, a cop and my sister, that's who was here." (John McKay, CP)

THE HAWK

Lightfoot takes to stage in comeback concert

It was a hero's welcome for Gordon Lightfoot as the legendary singer-songwriter returned to the stage in 2004. Lightfoot played five songs including his classic hit, "If You Could Read My Mind", at a benefit concert for the victims of a summer flood in the Ontario city of Peterborough. The folk legend hadn't formally sang in public since he nearly died after an artery ruptured in his abdomen during a weekend of concerts in his hometown of Orillia, Ont. Lightfoot, 65, spent three months in hospital recovering, including five weeks in a coma.

Ronnie Hawkins introduced the folk troubadour by calling him "legend of legends, icon of icons. (He's) one of the great talents of the world." Hawkins, who lives on Stoney Lake, northeast of Peterborough and helped organize the concert, also beat death in 2002 after being diagnosed with pancreatic cancer. "We're a tag team," said a jovial Hawkins, his arm wrapped around Lightfoot. "Gordon has the talent and I've got good looks and a beautiful body. We're unstoppable."

◀ Ronnie Hawkins and his wife Wanda joke backstage with Gordon Lightfoot. (Clifford Skarstedt/*Peterborough Examiner*)

Canada's latest late-night host loses his job

For late-night TV talk show hosts, Canada is a tough market. In 2004 Mike Bullard found himself the latest victim of American gabbers and ratings grabbers such as David Letterman, Conan O'Brien and Jay Leno.

Bullard, who made a well-publicized jump from CTV to Global television only to see his ratings plummet, had his show cancelled in March 2004. "It's just that the ratings weren't very good," said David Hamilton, Global's vice-president of publicity. Bullard made no public comment.

Bullard had debuted on Global in November 2003 to great fanfare, five months after his high-profile departure from rival CTV where for six years his show aired in prime time on the Comedy Network and late night on the main network.

Critics offered several reasons for the gruff comic's slide. First, there was the five-month wait to return to the air, during which time many of his fans became hooked on CTV's replacement, *The Daily Show* with Jon Stewart, a news parody import from the U.S. Then there was Bullard's open criticism of his former employer.

Bullard was not the first late-night host in Canadian TV to get the axe. He joins a list that includes Peter Gzowski, Ralph Benmergui and Alex Barris. (John McKay, CP)

▲ Glenn Murray, co-author of *Walter the Farting Dog*, holds a copy of the book and a *People* magazine showing actor Jack Nicholson reading from it. (Stephen MacGillivray/*Fredericton Daily Gleaner*)

Smelly dog sells books

It's an ill wind that blows no good, but the noxious emissions that wafted from the rear end of a dog named Walter have brought nothing but fame to his proud Fredericton family and fortune to the authors who immortalized him.

Walter the Farting Dog, and its sequel, *Trouble at the Yard Sale*, sat at the tops of bestseller lists for weeks, at one point occupying both the No. 1 and the No. 2 spots on the *New York Times'* list for illustrated children's books.

The books were based on a real-life dog who lived in Fredericton in the 1970s and '80s. "He suffered from flatulence," said owner Iris Burden. "It gagged everybody. When he walked away, he'd be doing it and he would turn around thinking he was being followed. And he was, by an odour and blue smoke."

Writers William Kotzwinkle and Glenn Murray lived in Fredericton in those days and came to know Walter and thought a kid's book based on the malodorous mutt would be popular. But it was turned down by publishers for 10 years because of its off-colour subject matter. Then North Atlantic Books of Berkeley, Calif., decided to publish it in 2001. The 40-page book, illustrated by Audrey Colman, was an instant hit and a sequel wasn't far behind. And there will be more. The book has been translated into several languages.

Walter the Farting Dog tells the story of a pooch rescued from the pound by a family who then want to return him because of his chronic flatulence. His liability turns into an asset when two burglars break into the home and Walter foils the heist with a particularly nasty gas attack.

"There's a flippant side to Walter but there's other stuff going on as well," says Murray, an educator who still lives in Fredericton and has been involved in the New Brunswick school system for years. "Whenever I read to kids, it's a great chance to talk about acceptance. Everyone has problems but that doesn't mean there's anything wrong with them . . . And it's about turning liabilities into assets." (Chris Morris, CP)

2004: Not the music industry's greatest year

In March, the Canadian Recording Industry Association, which represents record labels, lost a bid to get access from Internet service providers to the names and addresses of people that it believed were uploading music to the Internet for others to copy freely. Judge Konrad von Finckenstein of Federal Court gave downloading music from the Internet the green light, saying that uploading songs to shared folders on a home computer was permissible under the law because the songs weren't actively being distributed to others. He compared the action to allowing photocopy machines in public libraries that are filled with copyrighted books.

Von Finckenstein said that under privacy laws the music association had no legal entitlement to the identities, which are hidden by online aliases. The association appealed the decision, important to the music industry because without names it can't go ahead with lawsuits against people who make copies of songs without paying for them. The association argues the Copyright Act gives a song owner the sole right to authorize its reproduction.

Then in June, the Supreme Court of Canada ruled that Internet service providers don't have to pay royalties to composers and performers for music downloaded or heard via online radio by web customers. In a 9-0 judgement, the court said companies providing wide access to the web are merely "intermediaries" who are not bound by federal copyright legislation.

At issue was an effort by the Society of Composers, Authors and Music Publishers of Canada to force Internet service providers to pay a tariff for music accessed in the online world whether downloaded or streamed for online radio. The case dated back to 1995, a few years before Napster revolutionized the way fans get their hands on tunes. The judges noted, however, that Canadian copyright law is archaic and invited Parliament to update it to meet the needs of the modern information age. Canadian judges are struggling to apply legal principles first enunciated in the 1880s to "technologies undreamed of by those early legislators," the court said.

The court left the door open for recording artists to sue specific websites that distribute their music without authorization. Society lawyer Paul Spurgeon said the group would be proceeding with setting royalties.

Luc Lavoie, vice-president of Quebecor Inc., which owns Internet service provider Videotron, said ISPs have been wrongly targeted by music companies. "There's no difference between doing this [piracy] or using the telephone," said Lavoie. "You cannot blame the telephone company because criminals are speaking to one another over the phone." (Angela Pacienza, CP)

Canadian Idol winner Kalan Porter, of Medicine Hat, Alta., performs after winning the competition on September 16.

Opposite page: Theresa Sokyrka and Porter perform the show's opening number. (Frank Gunn/CP)

Canadian Idol soars to top of TV's most-watched list

Critics called it hokey, but that didn't stop CTV's *Canadian Idol* from becoming the biggest phenomenon to hit the Canadian pop culture scene in recent history. In 2003, its first year, it became the country's most watched homegrown English TV show with an average of 2 million viewers tuning in each week. By Year 2, CTV said, 3.3 million viewers were watching as an 18-year-old college student from a ranch near Medicine Hat, Alta., won the national singing contest.

The concept, which has swept the world as countries copy the format, is a musical bakeoff as young wannabe singers compete to see who can attract the most votes by phone or text-message from the at-home audience. Once the final round is reached, one competitor is eliminated each week until only one is left holding the microphone. The winner gets a recording contract.

For its second Canadian season, an estimated 9,000 aspiring singers auditioned for a chance to be one of the final 32 contestants who actually make it to the televised portion of the contest. Kalan Porter, who was studying commerce at Medicine Hat College when he auditioned, won the second Canadian Idol crown, beating jazz-pop songstress Theresa Sokyrka, 23, of Saskatoon. "I thought I wanted to take a year off to do some music. I guess this is doing some music," the curly-haired newbie shrugged with a big grin, as a horde of handlers from record label BMG looked on from the sidelines.

Critics loved to deride the show as a glorified karaoke competition, but the series became a mammoth event for its fans, especially for those in the hometowns of the finalists. Thousands gathered at arenas in Medicine Hat, Alta., and Saskatoon, Sask. to cheer on Porter and Sokyrka. The scenes were reminiscent of the fan hysteria reached during Stanley Cup playoffs. (Angela Pacienza, CP)

Toronto was inundated with the glitz and glamour of the film world as the stars crashed the city during its annual film festival in September. Far left: Kate Bosworth arrives for the gala screening of her film, *Beyond the Sea*. (Aaron Harris/CP) Middle: Jamie Foxx arrives for the gala screening of *Ray*. (Aaron Harris/CP) Left: Helen Hunt sports an "I love Toronto" T-shirt at a news conference promoting her film, *A Good Woman*. (J.P. Moczulski/CP) Below: Nick Nolte keeps cool with a fan at a news conference for the film *Clean*. (Aaron Harris/CP)

Toronto Film Festival

Raymond Sobeski, left, celebrates his $30-million lottery win with Alan Berdowski of Ontario Lotteries and Gaming on April 1. (Rene Johnston/*Toronto Star*)

PART 10

Fairly Odd News

Canada's biggest lottery winner shy about collecting winnings

The first news report was strange enough—a man who won the single largest jackpot in Canadian lottery history waited almost a year to collect his money. But within days after Raymond Sobeski finally came forward to receive his $30 million in Super 7 winnings, the story got even more bizarre.

Sobeski, of Princeton near Brantford, Ont., told a news conference on April Fool's Day that he was single and had no one special in his life. He said he hadn't told a soul about the win because he wanted to "make a plan and get some professional help and not be too concerned about the interest, because there's more important things than that."

It turned out he did have more important things to be concerned about. Court documents surfaced suggesting Sobeski had been married twice and divorced at least once. The most recent wife, Nynna Ionson, said they were still married—and Sobeski never told her about the ticket, despite the fact they had been together the night before he collected his cheque. Ionson, who had four children, also told reporters the two did not live together; she lived in subsidized housing in Woodstock, Ont., relying on donated food to get by. At last word, she had turned to the courts to help her get a share of the big win.

▲ "Professor Popsicle" Gordon Giesbrecht films a how-to video on water rescue at the Pan Am Water Ski Park in Winnipeg in 2001. (Ken Gigliotti/*Winnipeg Free Press*)

popsicle

Winnipeg's Professor Popsicle takes icy plunge on Letterman's talk show

In what might be considered an extreme stupid human trick, a Winnipeg university professor spent more than 15 minutes in a tank of ice water for an appearance on TV's *Late Night with David Letterman.*

But for Gordon Giesbrecht, a thermo-physiology professor known at the University of Manitoba as Prof. Popsicle, only the TV cameras and New York location made his trip to the verge of hypothermia unusual.

"Whoa, Dave, it's cold," Giesbrecht said, coughing and red-faced just moments after he took a step and plunged through a crust of ice-cubes into the tank. Wearing only a light winter outfit, he stayed in the water tank as the countdown clock ticked past 16 minutes. After about five minutes, the host checked in with Giesbrecht. "I was actually pretty uncomfortable before, but now I'm numb," he said.

The professor has built a reputation for being able to lower his body temperature dozens of times while pursuing his research into the effects of cold on the human body. He agreed to the TV stunt because it would allow him to prove to a wide audience that a fall through the ice isn't fatal within minutes.

killer bees

Bees kill heifer on southwestern Ontario farm

It was like something out of an Alfred Hitchcock movie. But instead of birds, bees terrorized a southwestern Ontario farm near Merlin, killing a cow and chasing a farmer into his home.

Veterinarian Dr. John Leonn treated the pregnant heifer, stung numerous times, with anti-inflammatory drugs but the animal died. It was believed she disturbed a hive while grazing.

Local beekeeper Michael Dodok, was surprised to learn of the incidents. "That must have been one heck of an aggressive hive," he said. (*Chatham Daily News*)

high living

Back-country break-in artist eats foods, drinks booze, then tidies up

A modern-day Goldilocks—with a penchant for booze instead of porridge—broke into cabins on a mountain in West Vancouver in 2004. The brazen back-country burglar consumed cabin owners' food and liquor and slept in their beds.

At least seven cabin owners reported break-ins. One found someone else's empty Old Stock beer cans inside his cabin. Another reported about $100 in canned food and liquor stolen, with $50 inexplicably left on the kitchen counter. Yet another said someone had slept in his bed, and then re-made it. Sometimes dishes were washed and tables cleaned but nothing stolen, even though several desirable items were within reach. (*Vancouver Province*)

UFOs

Maybe they like maple syrup: Number of UFOs being spotted in Canada increases

From a translucent, saucer-shaped object in British Columbia to mysterious lights buzzing motorists in New Brunswick, Canadians claimed to see a lot more unidentified flying objects in the first half of 2004 than they did in the same period a year earlier.

More than 400 sightings were reported as of August, compared with the 300 spotted during the same time in 2003, said Ufology Research of Manitoba in Winnipeg, which investigates eyewitness accounts. The number put Canada on pace to top the 2003 record of 670, said Chris Rutkowski of Ufology. He wasn't sure why the numbers were rising, but suspected it might be linked to public awareness of recent exploratory missions to intriguing planets such as Mars and Saturn.

One of Rutkowski's favourite sightings was in Caraquet, N.B., where odd pairs of lights were spotted in January above a highway. "One person reported seeing something with two or three lights and some sort of structure attached to it," Rutkowski said. "That area seemed to be quite a UFO hot spot this winter."

Most UFO sightings can be attributed to natural phenomena or human activity, he said.

"There's a small percentage that we simply don't have explanations for. There's probably life out there somewhere, but whether it can come all the way here is the big question."

earthworms

Too many earthworms threaten alpine environment near Calgary

An abundance of earthworms has threatened the fragile alpine environment in Kananaskis Country west of Calgary. "It's something that few people right now understand or appreciate," said Steve Donelon, parks ecologist for Alberta Community Development. "Any time you have some kind of invasive species, we're concerned about the impact it might have on other aspects of the ecosystem."

The fear is the slimy creatures are overrunning the thin soil of the Rocky Mountains. Earthworms may be good in gardens, but they are hard on ecosystems that aren't used to their presence, said Karen Yee, a University of Calgary biologist. University researchers recruited volunteers to help determine just how serious the problem was by digging in and monitoring the presence of the earthworms.

The worms first appeared in the Kananaskis area in the late 1980s. They were likely brought there on the hooves of horses used by tourists. Prior to that, glaciers that once covered the Rockies killed off any earthworms. (*Calgary Herald, Calgary Sun*)

▲ A squirrel makes away with a golfer's ball at the Riverside Golf Course in Edmonton. (Brian Gavriloff/*Edmonton Journal*)

golf squirrel

Speedy golf-ball-stealing rodents drive Edmonton golfers squirrelly

Forget the water hazards and sand traps. Golfers at Edmonton's Riverside Golf Course reported they had to watch the fairways carefully at Holes No. 10 and 18 where speedy squirrels were filching golf balls. "Some people come in after a round and say they've lost four or five balls," said apprentice golf pro Dillon Wilder.

The squirrel thieves were so common that Riverside established a special course rule: players could replace their balls without penalty if fellow golfers agreed where it landed on the fairway.

The squirrels weren't burying the balls, but taking them up trees and stuffing them in magpie nests. One theory was the rodent robbers were trying to drive the birds away. A ball hawk once reportedly recovered 250 balls from a single tree.

Officials at the golf course, in the heart of the city's river valley, welcomed ideas for ending the squirrels' antics but nothing "nutty," said Wilder. (*Edmonton Journal*)

runaway cat

Woman reunited with runaway cat after 18 years on the lam

After someone mistakenly let her cat out 18 years ago, Leslie Dumas of Selkirk, Man., thought she would never see her precious pet again. Then the Winnipeg Humane Society called and she was finally reunited with her long-lost Seagull.

"How long do most cats live? He survived a fire, he survived being lost for all these years to finally get back together with me," said Dumas, a 41-year-old restaurant owner whose cat was identified by a tattoo in its ear.

After her own home was destroyed by fire, Dumas was living in her boyfriend's mother's house outside Selkirk in the winter of 1986 when the cat ran away. "We searched, we put ads in the paper, we went up the streets calling and calling. Eighteen years later I almost forgot about him," Dumas said.

Dumas figured the 20-year-old cat, blind with cataracts, malnourished and dehydrated, must have found a home for most of his lost years before recently hitting the skids. (*Winnipeg Sun*)

butter!

This butter tastes too good to go down the drain

A dairy in Sussex, N.B., creamed the competition at the Olympics of butter. Dairytown Products topped 1,300 entries from 19 countries in March 2004 to win gold at a competition to pick the world's best butter.

It was a record year for entries in the competition, which is held every two years and hosted by the Wisconsin Cheesemakers Association. Dairytown's butter was also voted Canada's best for five years running at the Royal Agricultural Winter Fair in Toronto.

The secret to churning out the best-tasting butter in the world is a mix of having access to fresh milk and having experienced employees. About one-third of New Brunswick's 280 dairy farms are in the Sussex area, so Dairytown doesn't have to go far to get fresh milk. (*New Brunswick Telegraph-Journal*)

cheesy sentence

Man caught stealing cheese ordered to produce a painting for the courts

A homeless artist caught stealing a $3.89 piece of cheese received an usual sentence: he was ordered to produce a painting for an Ottawa courthouse. Following a guilty plea for the attempted pilfering of a package of Black Diamond marble cheddar, Matthew Cardinal, 37, was sentenced to create the work of art and serve six months of probation.

Justice Paul Belanger ordered the artist to deliver the painting to the courthouse for permanent display. "This place could use some improvement in the decor," said Crown prosecutor Kevin Phillips. "I just hope no one steals the thing." (*Ottawa Sun*)

backyard grenade

Grenade discovered in Yellowknife backyard detonated by military bomb squad

Yellowknife is a long way from any warfronts. That made the discovery of a military grenade buried in a backyard in the Northern Canadian town a bit of a head-scratcher.

A team of military explosives experts were called in from Cold Lake, Alta., to deal with the grenade that Graham Watts found while helping his daughter Annike clear brush and trash from around her mobile home. "It was dirty and he didn't realize it wasn't a rock until he dusted it off," Annike said.

The explosives experts took the pineapple-shaped object to a sand pit and blew it up with plastic explosives. They determined it was a Mark II grenade, which was used during the Second World War, in Korea and Vietnam.

PART 11
Passages

Betty Oliphant, founder of the National Ballet School, helps a student in 1984. (John Mahler/*Toronto Star*)

Alex Barris

Gerald Bouey, 83 Bouey, governor of the Bank of Canada from 1973 to 1987, was described by a successor, David Dodge, as a "consummate governor, a man of enormous intellect and integrity" who was also warm and funny. It is likely the thousands of Canadians who were unable to meet their mortgage payments in 1981 when Bouey cranked up interest rates to record levels in an effort to squelch inflation did not have the same fond memories. Bouey aggressively imposed sky-high interest rates, reflecting moves in the United States as central bankers toiled to squeeze out inflationary expectations among businesses and consumers. **Reva Brooks, 90** Born in Toronto, Brooks, a photographer, moved to San Miguel de Allende in Mexico in 1947 with her artist-husband Leonard Brooks. The couple played a leading role in making San Miguel de Allende a famous art colony. Brooks' photographs of Mexicans soon came to the attention of leading U.S. photographers

Alex Barris, 81 Although an American by birth, Barris was a staple of the early days of CBC-TV. He hosted the *Barris Beat*, a musical-variety series produced and directed by Norman Jewison that shared a name with his *Toronto Telegram* column, from 1956 to 1957. Barris was also a panelist on the venerable *Front Page Challenge* as well as the host of several other game shows. One critic once described him as "a clever ad-libber, a probing interviewer, a suitably obtuse straight man, a ham and many other things."

Gerald Bouey

Edward Weston and Ansel Adams. In the mid-1950s the New York Museum of Modern Art included her in its Family of Man exhibit, one of the most famous photographic shows ever. In 1975 the San Francisco Museum of Art selected her as one of the top 50 women photographers in history.

Norman Campbell, 80 A producer, writer and composer, Campbell was known as one of the founding geniuses of Canadian television. Born in Los Angeles, he first joined CBC Vancouver as a radio producer in 1948. Four years later in Toronto he produced some of CBC's first trail-blazing telecasts. He won an Emmy award in 1970 for his ballet production of *Cinderella* and another in 1972 for *Sleeping Beauty*. He is perhaps best known for co-writing the musical version of *Anne of Green Gables* along with Don Harron that has played to summer audiences in Prince Edward Island ever since. Campbell also worked in the United States, directing TV specials for Diana Ross, Bing Crosby, Frank Sinatra and Andy Williams, as well as episodes of the *Mary Tyler Moore Show* and *All in the Family*.

Micheline Charest, 51 With her husband Ronald Weinberg, Charest co-founded the award-winning film company Cinar Inc., which specialized in quality children's shows such as *Caillou* and *Arthur*. She was a leading Quebec business woman and a star in the North American entertainment industry. But Charest died with a cloud over her integrity as a result of governance and legal scandals that erupted in 2000 at Cinar. And her death, during plastic surgery, also led to headlines and controversy over why such a successful woman felt the need to undergo the procedure. The financial scandals almost wiped out the company's stock price and led to its delisting on stock markets. Charest and Weinberg were ousted and Cinar was sold to a Toronto investors' group. Charest once said she was "getting really tired of being referred to as 'disgraced founders'" by the media. "Before I became 'disgraced' in the eyes of the sensationalist press, I was simply a founder who worked the better part of 20 years building a great company."

Frank Cotroni, 72 Cotroni was a reputed crime boss who rose to prominence during Montreal's Mafia heyday of the 1950s, '60s and '70s. But at his elaborate funeral in Montreal's Little Italy district, Cotroni's convictions for manslaughter and

Micheline Charest

Frank Cotroni

cookbook author. Doug Creighton, 75 Creighton's career as a newsman began in the mailroom of the *Toronto Telegram* in 1948. He eventually ended up in the *Telegram's* managing editor's office. A day after the paper folded in 1971, the first edition of the *Toronto Sun,* created by Creighton and some of his *Telegram* colleagues, rolled off the presses. Critics gave the feisty tabloid 30 days. Under Creighton's leadership, the paper became a national chain, including *Sun*s in Edmonton, Calgary and Ottawa. Creighton was a boss who knew his many employees by name—as well as the names of their spouses and kids—and inspired them with his warmth, wit, charisma and vision. And he was always up for a good party.

drug smuggling were largely forgotten as friends and family hailed him as a kind and giving man. Cotroni, along with brothers Vic and Pepe, were linked to New York's powerful Bonanno crime organization and allegedly controlled several Quebec rackets. Frank Cotroni spent much of his adult life in prison but had another side to him as well—he was a published

Doug Creighton

Frances Hyland, 77 In a career that spanned more than 50 years, Hyland starred in and directed numerous productions at both the Stratford and Shaw festivals and also appeared in regional theatre, films and television. After graduating from the University of Saskatchewan in 1948, Hyland won a scholarship to study at the Royal Academy of Dramatic Art in England. She made her professional debut in 1950 in a London production of *A Streetcar Named Desire*. In 1954 she was brought back to Canada by Tyrone Guthrie, founding artistic director of the Stratford Festival, to appear as Isabella opposite James Mason in *Measure for Measure*. Richard Monette, Stratford's artistic director, said Hyland "dealt with the world, and all its problems and joys, through her art. She was a great lady of the theatre."

Eric Kierans, 90 Although Eric Kierans became best known in his later years for being part of Peter Gzowski's political panel on the *Morningside* show on CBC Radio, he had a long and varied career in the trenches of politics. He was a headstrong Canadian economic nationalist who moved from Quebec politics to become a minister in Pierre Trudeau's government. He ran for the federal Liberal leadership in 1968 but was defeated by Trudeau, who named him postmaster general and then communications minister. Kierans resigned from cabinet in April 1971 and left politics in 1972, opposed to key economic policies that included rising government expenditures.

Brian Linehan, 58 Linehan, a puckish TV personality, first brought his authoritative enthusiasm to interview chores at *City Lights*, the showbiz program that began airing in 1973 on CHUM Television's then-fledgling Citytv channel in Toronto. Linehan's meticulous research and in-depth questioning quickly gave him that reputation as an interviewer par excellence. "I'm starting to sweat with the amount of info he's got on me," actor Dustin Hoffman once said.

Keith Magnuson, 56 Magnuson was a tough, tenacious defenceman during his 11-year career with the NHL's Chicago Blackhawks from 1969 to 1980. The Saskatoon native was not an offensive threat but he was an intimidating presence on Chicago's blue-line with 1,442 career penalty minutes. "Keith didn't have the greatest hockey skills but he more than made up for it with hard work, his attitude, desire and dedication for the game," said Cliff Koroll, a longtime friend and

Eric Kierans

Keith Magnuson

teammate. Magnuson also coached the Blackhawks from 1980 to '82, compiling a 49-57-26 record.

Harrison McCain, 76 McCain was a New Brunswick farm boy who became a world-scale industrialist and the king of the frozen french fry. He and his brother Wallace transformed the sleepy farming community of Florenceville, N.B., into the command centre for one of the world's largest frozen food companies, responsible for frying up one-third of the planet's frozen french fries. McCain Foods Ltd., founded in 1956 by Wallace, Harrison and two brothers, grew to employ more than 18,000 people at 55 plants around the world, with billions in annual sales. Some regarded Harrison as a brash and un-pleasant egomaniac; others as a true captain of industry. For journalists, he was a terror to interview. When asked to describe the secret of his success, he barked back, "Right place, right time. Next question."

In the mid-1990s a bitter succession feud between Harrison and Wallace boiled over into the courts and the public domain. Wallace was eventually ousted from his job and ended up orchestrating a takeover of Maple Leaf Foods with his sons. Although there was no public reconciliation, Frank McKenna, the former premier of New Brunswick and a close friend

Harrison McCain, right

of the McCains, said the two became closer again before Harrison died. Jack McClelland, 81 McClelland was one of Canada's most influential publishers. At his memorial service, his friends and writers fondly recalled the former head of McClelland and Stewart for his flamboyant publicity stunts, fierce devotion to all things Canadian, and a penchant for imbibing vodka with authors. Margaret Atwood, Pierre Berton, Leonard Cohen, Mordecai Richler, Farley Mowat and Peter C. Newman all rose to fame under the stewardship of McClelland, who was a strong voice for Canadian culture and a national identity. He launched several series such as the New Canadian Library paperbacks and the Canadian Centenary Series. "Jack's passing marks an end of a flamboyant triangles and rectangles. Moe Norman, 75 Norman, of Kitchener, Ont., became a phenomenon in the amateur golfing circuit in the 1950s and '60s, renowned for his unusual swing and amazing accuracy. Regarded by many as the best striker ever, Norman captured 13 Canadian Tour events and played for Canada at the 1971 World Cup. His swing was so numbingly consistent that even in competition he would joke around, frustrating playing partners by hitting the ball off eight-inch tees, wooden tee markers and Coke bottles. The eccentric Norman often played with his pants up over his ankles and a stained shirt. He also sometimes wore as

Jack McClelland

period in Canadian publishing," said longtime friend Berton. Guido Molinari, 70 Born in Montreal, Molinari was an inventive abstract painter who was a dominant figure in Canadian art for more than five decades. His philosophy about painting was simple. "There is no such thing as a colour, there are only colour harmonies," Molinari once said. "A given colour exists only in its shape and dimensions—and in its correlation with other colours." During various periods in his painting, he used only black and white, stripes or

Moe Norman

Claude Ryan

many as five wristwatches at once to ensure he had the correct time. Betty Oliphant, 85 Oliphant became the founding principal of Canada's National Ballet School in Toronto, eight years after moving to the country from her native England. She was the school's artistic director from 1975 until 1989. She had a lasting influence on Canadian ballet, having trained many of the country's finest dancers, including Rex Harrington and Karen Kain. Toni Onley, 75 The little float plane that enabled Onley to bring remote corners of Canada's West Coast to the world through his paintings was also the vehicle that led to his death. The renowned watercolourist crashed his plane into the Fraser River while practising landings and takeoffs. "His contribution was to create this kind of very good technique of British watercolour that he has in fact transformed for his own end," said curator Denise Leclerc of the National Gallery of Canada in Ottawa. Claude Ryan, 79 The Quebec Liberal leader was best known across Canada as the cerebral leader of the provincial federalist forces that defeated René Lévesque in the 1980 Quebec referendum on separatism. Long before his political career, Ryan was well-known in Quebec as the influential writer and editor with *Le Devoir*. He dispensed wisdom to both

sides of any debate and wielded his pen like a sword. After the federalists won the 1980 vote, Ryan did not reach out in conciliation to defeated sovereignists, about 40 per cent of Quebec's population, but continued to preach about the importance of the federalist victory. One year later, he lost a provincial election he was expected to win in a landslide. He never became premier, but did serve as a cabinet minister before retiring from politics in 1994. Mitchell Sharp, 92 Sharp personified the term elder statesman. At the age of 82, after a half-century of public service and long after his contemporaries

Mitchell Sharp

Robert Stanfield

had left politics, Sharp signed on as a $1-a-year per-sonal adviser to then-prime minister Jean Chrétien. And he kept at it into his 90s. Sharp served in Lester Pearson's government but his heyday was in the cab-inet of Pierre Trudeau. Friendly, polite and casual in private, he was a tough, no-nonsense negotiator when he had to be. While he was foreign affairs minister, the government established relations with China, shifted its policies regarding the United States, halved its military commitment to the North Atlantic Treaty Organization and began new dialogues with Europe and Japan. Robert Stanfield, 89 As premier of Nova Scotia in the 1950s and '60s, Stanfield was one of Canada's most successful provincial politicians. Then he became the Conservative Opposition leader in Ottawa and Trudeaumania put him into the his-tory books as the best prime minister Canada never had. Born into the famous underwear family of Truro, N.S., Stanfield had a face as craggy as the coast of his native province. Massive eyebrows guarded his deep-set brown eyes. Dark-rimmed glasses added to his scholarly appearance. His slow speaking style often obscured his quick wit. But it was a CP news photographer's picture snapped dur-ing the 1974 federal election campaign that indelibly typecast Stanfield. During an impromptu game of catch on the airport tarmac in North Bay, Ont., he was captured dropping the football. The contrast to the athletic figure of Liberal Prime Minister Pierre Trudeau could not have been starker. Stanfield couldn't catch a break in Ottawa and he frequently joked that he could walk on water and the next day's headlines would say: Bob Stanfield Can't Swim. But he was not afraid to take controversial positions. His proposal for wage and price controls in 1974 and his support for two official languages grated on

Hugh Charles Trainor

in the process found a career for himself as a politician. First elected to Edmonton city council in 1977, he later famously defeated then-premier Don Getty in the 1989 provincial election to serve as a Liberal. Fay Wray, 96 Wray won everlasting fame as the damsel held atop the Empire State Building by the giant ape in the 1933 film classic *King Kong*. Although the role obscured her other notable films, the Alberta-born actress once said she learned not to resent the campy classic. "I don't fight it anymore," she said in 1963. "I realize that it is a classic and I am pleased to be associated with it." Born near Cardston in rural Alberta, Wray's parents moved to the United States when she was three, eventually settling in Los Angeles. As a teenager she haunted studio casting offices and won an occasional bit role. After appearing in Erich von Stroheim's 1928 silent *The Wedding March*, Wray became a much-employed leading lady. In 1933, she appeared in 11 films, including *King Kong*.

some Tories. He resigned as Conservative leader in 1976, after losing three elections to Trudeau. Hugh Charles Trainor, 87 A Royal Canadian Air Force fighter pilot in the Second World War, Trainor shot down 10 enemy aircraft during the Second World War—more than twice the number needed to be considered an ace. Trainor was shot down and captured twice. The first time he was captured, he managed to escape. But in September 1944 he was taken prisoner and held until the end of the war. The native of Prince Edward Island was later decorated with the Distinguished Service Order, and the Distinguished Flying Cross and bar for his wartime service. Percy Wickman, 63 In 1964, while unloading box cars at work, a door fell on Wickman, breaking his back. The injury took away the use of his legs, but gave him a cause—as a leading advocate for disabled people. Wickman helped found the Alberta Committee of Citizens with Disabilities and

Fay Wray

The Canadian Press
The Last Word. First.

Dear Reader,

This publication is a collection of our most prized images. Some of the images you may have seen before in your local newspaper. Others you may be seeing for the first time.

    High-quality prints of many of the photographs in this book may be purchased for personal use. Prints may be ordered in two sizes, 8 x 10 inches and 11 x 14 inches, unframed.

    A complete caption will also be provided with the photo.

To order prints using our secure online
order form, please visit http://www.cp.org/prints

We accept Visa, MasterCard and American Express.

You can also mail in your order.
Please include the following information:

-Please include the book title, page number
 and a brief description of the image
-The size and number of prints of each photo
-Your credit card type, number and expiry date
-Your return address

Mail to:
  CP Images
  36 King Street East
  Toronto, Ontario, M5C 2L9

PRINT PRICES:
8 x 10 - $55.00 for the first print,
        $25.00 for the second print* and
        $15.00 for each additional print*

11 x 14 - $80.00 for the first print,
        $35.00 for the second print* and
        $25.00 for each additional print*

We will add applicable federal and provincial taxes to each order. Prices include shipping.

* of the same image